Survival Theory

Eugene Randall

Comments, questions, or to request permission for academic citation, contact the author at
survivalinstruction@gmail.com

Warnings

Although the author and publisher have made every effort to ensure this book was correct at press time, the author and publisher do not assume and hereby disclaim any liability to any party for any loss, damage, or disruption caused by errors or omissions, whether such errors or omissions result from negligence, accident, or any other cause.

This book is not intended as a substitute for the medical advice of physicians. The reader should consult a physician in matters relating to his/her health and particularly with respect to any symptoms that may require diagnosis or medical attention.

The information in this book is meant to supplement, not replace, proper survival and firearms training. Any activity involving weapons, vehicles, tactical drills, military procedures, construction, wilderness, and environmental factors poses some inherent risk. The reader is advised to take full responsibility for their safety and know their limits. Before practicing the skills in this book, be sure that you are in full compliance with all laws, codes, and statutes, your equipment is well maintained, and do not take risks beyond your level of experience, aptitude, training, and comfort level.

Ensure that you follow all local, state, and federal laws. It is the sole responsibility of the reader to ensure he/she understands the laws in his/her location and does not violate the law in any way; ignorance of the law will not shield the reader from criminal prosecution or civil liability. The reader should consult an attorney for certain legal advice.

To my son and my daughter, who I love
with all my heart- Dad

Table of Contents

Introduction

How do you share helpful knowledge to both the beginner and intermediate survivalist, and still be relevant to the advanced survivalist? The answer is to simply say what you know and let the reader choose what is applicable. This book and all its pages is your property to do with as you will. If you are reading this you are an individualist in true form; you think and live on your own terms anyway. A look in the thesaurus shows there is no synonym for "survivalist."

My curriculum vitae (or resume) are two decades as a US Army infantryman, a lifetime hunting, fishing, and trapping, service in multinational units on three continents, service in three wars, and providing aid after multiple disasters. I have seen things that work and do not work; have lately heard things that are good ideas, and fairly often heard things that could be bad ideas. At this point in life I have lived and worked in wildernesses, remote locations, combat, and disaster areas almost as much as I've lived around "suburbia". The things I have seen certainly made an impression on me; and I suspect the pages that follow may make some impression on you as well.

This is not a manual. Most of these contents are very far from "step-by-step". There are already enough manuals out there and most of those seem to lose something in the clean organization of 1, 2, 3, and 4, complete. Neither is this a reference book, presuming to index exactly how to do mundane tasks. This *is* a collection of essays aimed at investigation for the outcome of survival. We will examine methods, equipment, approaches, concepts, techniques, and more in an effort to understand how to stay alive. We will further analyze why some things work in some circumstances but maybe not in other situations.

One list of disaster-type scenarios I reviewed had over 100 possible events. There are books which are dedicated to very specific types of emergencies or disasters...from being lost alone at sea, all the way to outlasting nuclear winter. If you believe a specific disaster is likely in your area, or believe you are prone to enduring a specific emergency, I encourage you to seek the material out there that goes in depth on those topics. However, within these pages, I made careful effort to never spend too much time on any single disaster scenario, based on the assertion that if you are ready for a major widespread catastrophe you can manage a generally localized disaster. From cover to cover here you will read mentioning of a wide assortment of emergencies and disasters.

Good luck on your survival and preparedness planning; may your canteens always be full. I believe the old army proverb that no matter how proficiently you may perform a skill or task, you have not mastered the thing until you have effectively taught it to other people. Thank you for reading, and please enjoy.

1. Tactics, Techniques, Procedures, Doctrine and etc

"Nine-tenths of tactics are certain, and taught in books: but the irrational tenth is like the kingfisher flashing across the pool, and that is the test of generals." T. E. Lawrence

The survival and prepping community is saturated with the use of "tactics, techniques, and procedures" (TTP's) to describe various tasks of all types. The same is true of "doctrine"; usually when someone claims a way to do something is "doctrine" it implies somehow this is the last word on the best way that it is done. Some other words are "strategy", and "tactical". Yet, somehow all these words get used interchangeably with no consistency until they lose usefulness in their individual meaning.

Is it important to know the difference between a tactic and a technique? Or what about understanding the difference between doctrine and procedures? Yes! If you are learning a skill set, practicing collective tasks, or planning an overall survival plan with specific large goals, it is important to at least be aware of how everything fits together. Knowing the definitions and concepts also makes it very easy to know who knows what they are talking about and who is just speaking in fashionable jargon.

Technique- A technique is <u>how you perform an individual task</u>. Most things in life have about 50 ways you can do it and all 50 ways are techniques. "If it doesn't work, it doesn't work; but if it does work it is a technique."

If someone shows you how to perform a speed-reload on a rifle, the way they did it is a technique. If it does work, that does not automatically mean it is the "right way" or the "best way", it just means it worked. There are probably many other ways to do it specifically to that rifle style, and each different technique will have advantages and disadvantages based on the situation. It is up to you to decide the techniques you like and what situations you will apply them in.

Procedure- A procedure is <u>an established way of performing a task or drill; either collectively or as an individual</u>. You will not hear folks mention the word *procedure* very often, but you will frequently hear folks talking about things that are procedures and inaccurately calling them everything else, from tactics to strategies to etc.

For our purpose, a procedure should be thought of as the way we accomplish something that has so many moving pieces that it must we standardized into a procedure so that it always works even when unknown variables are introduced. When done correctly, the procedure itself will become a drill that can be practiced.

Establishing procedures are important because they enable efficient tactics and they prevent us from making mistakes or forgetting steps under stress. Example: What we will do when encountering a group of refugees. Example: What we will do if _____ goes wrong. Other examples: Establishing how/who to consolidate the wounded; how to redistribute ammunition after a fight; how/when to change radio frequencies; when to inspect equipment; how to perform a hasty vehicle halt while traveling in a convoy.

Tactics- A tactic is <u>a way to place yourself where you can do the most damage to the enemy and he can do the least damage to you</u>. Pinning an enemy down with fire while your buddy flanks and overruns the enemy is a tactic. Or if multiple enemies are facing you and you reposition until only one enemy can engage you, forcing the other enemies to move from their preferred positions…that is a tactic.

When someone says, "This is the tactic I use to reload my rifle…" well that is not a tactic at all; that is a technique. How you aim a weapon or how you tie a knot is not a tactic.

What drives tactics? The simplest answer is that the terrain and situation will always drive the selection or use of a tactic within your doctrine. Example: We spotted the enemy patrol first and assumed concealed positions and performed a hasty ambush, until they reorganized and began to flank our positions and we were forced to retreat along the creek bed. (The tactics: patrolling, ambush, flanking, and retreat. Some folks would argue that reorganizing is a tactic, but it is a *procedure*.)

Doctrine- A doctrine is <u>a default set of beliefs about a concept</u>. Bottom line up front, doctrine is a very general thing based on your situation and abilities. It tells you what to do, but not how to do it. I have lost count of how many times I have heard someone explain, "Doctrine says to do this like this…" When you hear such, take it with a grain of salt and know that the person probably never read any doctrine about whatever it is they are talking about.

Doctrine will sound like: Establish security. Or it will say: Evacuate the wounded, place an obstacle, attack, retrograde, etc. Actual doctrine can be so vague as to say: Reload. Well there are a million ways to establish security or evacuate wounded or reload something. All these millions of ways will fall under tactics, techniques, and procedures (TTP's), and all that will be ultimately decided based upon the terrain and the situation. Doctrine just says which tactic is appropriate. Examples: Establish an ambush; break contact; defend in place.

Your situation and abilities drive your doctrine. You cannot have a doctrine that is beyond the capabilities of your **TTP's**. You cannot have an offensive doctrine, for example, if you do not have a group equipped to take on the enemy. Your group may be too weak to go on the offense, so you take on a <u>defensive</u> doctrine: obstacles, outposts, breaking contact, hasty ambushes, retrograde, etc. Maybe your group is strong and must be proactive to stay on top so you take on an <u>offensive</u> doctrine: raids, attacks, deliberate ambushes, long range patrols, etc. Maybe the weather/seasons impact your situation. Your doctrine will define what tactics, techniques, and procedures you disregard or adopt until things change. Example: During the winter season you have to stop doing raids because the mountain pass is closed. So you switch from the offense to defense until spring.

Strategy- A strategy is a <u>plan to achieve your overall goal</u>. A collection of tactics is used to form doctrine and doctrines help you build a strategy. Example 1: Our strategy to secure the farm will be a defensive doctrine made of trail ambushes during the day to stop enemy foot patrols and defend the interior perimeter at night to prevent raids. (This example strategy has one doctrine based on four tactics—two friendly defensive tactics countering two enemy offensive tactics.) You notice the enemy activity causes a defensive doctrine to develop. Example 2: Our strategy is to overwatch our bridge roadblocks to prevent the enemy from breaching in order to gain access to our community. (In this example an overwatch is the friendly tactic to counter the enemy tactic of breaching an obstacle; the overall strategy is defensive because it is to deny the enemy road/vehicle access to the town.) If you added in to pursue/counter-attack retreating enemy that failed to breach when they halt, you just added an offensive doctrine into your strategy. So Example 2 becomes a strategy of two doctrines.

Let's say your overall survival **Strategy** is that your group will use certain refugees to build a labor-force community with your group members as hierarchal leaders. That means you will need a **Doctrine** of selecting, assisting, winning over, integrating, training, housing/feeding, and governing certain desirable refugees while keeping away certain undesirable refugees and a Doctrine for protecting your resources. Your **TTP's** are the way you will conduct selecting, assisting, winning over, integrating, training, housing/feeding, and governing. Your **TTP's** is how you will choose to keep away undesirables. Protecting your resources is yet another **Doctrine**; either defense, offense, or both, which will be done using your preferred **TTP's**.

General order: Strategy → Doctrine → Tactics → Procedures → Techniques

Tactical (Tactically) - This may be the most misused word in the survival, outdoors, and prepping community. The misuse really started from advertising in the commercial sector. Military people transitioning into civilian sales brought the word with them and the advertisers went nuts with it. Everybody loves to label a thing as tactical, but almost nobody knows what it originally meant. Most folks assume it means a thing with some fuzzy relation to tactics and the military, but that is actually so generic as to be easily deceptive for marketing purposes.

Adjective: As a young infantryman, I learned that a piece of tactical equipment is, "an item so robust and simple that it will not fail or become too complicated to use under conditions so severe that it would make a less robust or more complicated item fail or be too complex to use."

The problem is that everything advertised as "tactical" is not even close to being that. Painting a cheap Pakistan knife green or dying cheap Chinese nylon black does not make it tactical; it is still just cheap junk that will not last through hard use. You may be better served by a regular hunting knife and old army surplus pouches.

A KA-BAR knife, RAT Cutlery, or Buck hunting knives (among a few other brands) are examples of tactical items; these are knives so tough that they will keep functioning in conditions that would make lesser knives unserviceable.

Another example I like to use is my Petzl headlamp. No it is not bulletproof and will not survive a plane crash like other tactical lights that come to mind, like Surfire or Blackhawk. And it is not bright enough to melt any retinas either. The Petzl is a bit flimsy and stepping on it may break it. But the Petzl is extremely easy to use, is straightforward in design, and lasts around 3 years of nearly nightly use on a set of lithium batteries. It can be used as a headlamp, tied to a tree branch or hung in a truck, can swiftly change to red or white light, can be brightened or dimmed, and has one waterproof switch that is simple to activate and adjust. It truly is a light that never gets too complex to use under any condition. As an infantryman I carried three or more lights and the Petzl was the one I kept closest, because it always worked easily and required no hands once it was on. For all the reasons mentioned, it qualified as "tactical" for me, even if it was not a super-bright, bomb-proof, miracle light.

Adverb: Go do that "tactically". Folks use the word a lot, and assume everyone knows what it means, but no one ever defines the word. Tactically just means "to do a thing in a way that gives you the most survivability".

You can walk across a road or you can crouch and hustle across the road. Walking upright makes you an easy target and crouching while you rush across makes you a more difficult target. So crouching and rushing across is more tactical.

Another example is walking in the woods. You can sling your rifle on your back and just stroll through the woods with no concern. Or you can carry your rifle in both hands, slung at a low ready, carefully moving through the woods while warily watching and listening for danger. Which way sounds like it has more survivability? That way is doing it tactically.

2. Planning

"Plans are worthless; planning is everything."
Dwight Eisenhower

The ability to plan is not a natural talent we get from birth. It is a skill that is learned through trials and errors. It is also a perishable skill that you have to keep doing or you will lose proficiency.

It is never too early to start planning. Not planning to survive is planning to die. Even if the disaster that unfolds and the aftermath are drastically different than what was anticipated, having at least a tentative template is way better than starting from scratch. The more we plan, the more it will become evident how much work we must really do to be ready.

One good thing about disaster plans is that many aspects are relatively redundant. Whether the anticipated disaster is a war, economic collapse, earthquake, asteroid, or any of the above, the requirements for defense, food, water, shelter, transportation, medical, trade, and etc will be inevitably alike. If you are ready for a super-virus outbreak, in theory you should be fairly prepared for a hurricane or EMP, with a few differences. A plan is simply essential to any level of preparedness.

Planning is one of those jobs that never really end; it is an ongoing process. If the world as we know it suddenly gets flipped on its side, obviously we then commit to our initial survival plan, but every day there will be occurrences or new requirements that arise which will necessitate further planning to execute. Not planning for success is the equivalent of planning to fail. To get the most bang for our buck, and to multiply our odds of success, planning ought to be systematic in order to minimize the chances of overlooking anything. PACE

<u>P</u>rimary plan

<u>A</u>lternate plan

<u>C</u>ontingency plan

<u>E</u>mergency plan

A *primary plan* is your Plan A. This is the preferred way we would like to execute what we are doing. Maybe we are going to the community 5 miles away to trade at the market or maybe we are going to the nearby lake to catch some fish...whatever it is we need a Plan A.

What would the primary plan include? First we have to identify the situation. What is our circumstances and condition? Is there a security threat and how bad is it? What are the terrain and environmental conditions? Next we define the goal or mission. Explain the intent. How far we must go, how long it should take, is is it better to go at night, who and what do we take, who do we leave back? These questions let us create a scheme of maneuver. Everything we are doing should be covered...how fast we will go, individual responsibilities and tasks assigned, coordination of when things should be done, rules of engagement, who is in charge, how we will communicate and signal, actions to take if we get a mechanical problem or get shot at, how we will handle casualties.

*This type of thing is **important** to plan and brief with a map or visual representation (like a sand table) so everyone involved can see what is where! Get a back brief from everyone, having them explain their part of the mission. Consider doing talk-through or walk-through rehearsals.

The *alternate plan* is the Plan B. If the situation changes and the primary plan is no longer an option, we use the alternate plan.

Is Plan A effected if it is night instead of day? Do things change if it is summer or winter? What about heavy rain or snow and ice? How does a sudden loss of fuel or electricity affect the plan? How does loss of a family member or other member affect us? How does a biological hazard affect the plan? Is the plan still viable if a highly contagious disease is a factor? Is there a major toxic condition, like a nuclear power plant, fuel refinery, or chemical factory nearby, that can make everything in one compass direction unsafe? Can flood waters make certain roads unusable?

Let us say Plan A was to travel on Highway 20, but at the last minute we learn that a bridge has collapsed; now we simply go to Plan B and depart on County Road 4124. Everything in the primary plan must be done in the alternate plan. Treat the alternate plan like a standalone plan and commit the same effort into the details and into briefing it.

Maybe Plan A was to leave work during an emergency in the car, but the car will not start. What is Plan B? We will always need Plan B ready, just like Plan A.

A *contingency plan* is where we really cover what to do if we have any deviations on the primary or alternate plans. A contingency should not be thought of as a Plan C. In fact, it is best to treat it as a sub-plan to either a Plan A or B. Let us say we arrive at the market and find out our group is too large to be welcome inside the community's perimeter; to enter only a maximum of 5 people from our group may enter until we have established a history of good rapport with the community members. If we find the request reasonable and still want to do some trading, now we need a contingency.

An easy contingency format is GOTWA (pronounced "got-wah"). This 5-point format will cover the basic gist, but there is no reason not to include more details. G—Where I'm going. O—Others going with me. T—Time I expect to return. W—What to do if I don't return and what I will do if you have to leave this area. A—Actions I will take if we get hit and actions you will take if you are hit.

I find that it is helpful to incorporate a soft version of GOTWA in my everyday life. Anytime I leave the house or go off on my own when the family is somewhere, I give a

GOTWA to the family and vice versa. The reason is that if we are ever in the aftermath of a disaster, GOTWA will already just be a good established habit.

The *emergency plan* is exactly what it sounds like. It is a detailed plan for what to do if the worst case turns real. Let us say we got wiped out on the road and the vehicles are destroyed; now the survivors must individually evade back to our own community.

How may we signal a warning home? Will we need a pre-positioned emergency cache? How will we navigate home? What are the major landmarks? What are the most concealed routes? How long may it take on foot? Are there documents we should burn? Do we destroy any of our equipment so it is not captured? At what point will the community send a rescue party and where should they be looking? What pre-established symbols can we leave (stacked rocks, blazes on trees, rope with knots, broken sticks, etc) for the rescue party, to tell them what we are doing (danger/beware, how many, which way headed, what time/day was here, where we will rally)?

3. Science of the Defense

"The home to everyone is to him his castle and fortress, as well as for his defense against injury and violence, as for repose."
Edward Coke

I am not talking about self-defense, but the actual defense of a structure, piece of ground, or a position. If you have never defended a piece of terrain or a building, most of the things that seem simple turn out not to be, and most of the things that would seem straightforward turn out to be not very basic. Simply leaving a few people with guns may be some deterrence, but it will not likely stop a deliberate attack or coordinated raid.

What are some things we may need to defend? Our home place, a settlement, a food/water source, a fuel source, a community, a bridge, a boundary, a key piece of terrain, a roadblock, or livestock are all just a few things we may find we want to defend. The "why" is not really important; what matters is if the need arises we should know how to successfully defend it.

For our purposes, let us assume we are doing a perimeter defense. The basics are the same and if you can defend a perimeter, then you can defend all else.

A successful defense must be redundant and in depth. A highly successful defense is steadily improved as time goes by. Some things a defense should include: Obstacles; Early Warning; Overwatch; Primary/Alternate Fighting Positions; Mutual Supporting Firing Positions; Interlocking Fields of Fire; and a Mobile Reserve.

<u>Obstacles</u>: These can be natural, man-made, or a combination of both. An obstacle should be used with one of two goals; either to stop the enemy or channel him into a kill zone. Just remember obstacles work like grenades: both ways.

Sometimes you may be able to completely halt an enemy force by blocking all the avenues of approach, such as using rockslides, ditches, and tree falls to plug a mountain pass, or by closing a bridge by plugging it with heavy rubble and wreckage. Other times the terrain will not allow total closing; in this case you create paths of less resistance that guide the enemy into open ground.

Wire (as in concertina wire, razor wire, and barbed wire/tangle-foot) should not be overlooked. Wire is cheap, has an indefinite shelf life, is easy to place, and can be very hard to negotiate in an attack. Enough wire can even stop vehicles; just ask any old mechanized soldiers if they have ever saw a tank stopped by concertina wire caught in the sprockets. Stringing wire over and around rockslides, ditches, and tree falls make them that much more of a pain to attempt to breach. Big nests of tangled wire dropped in creeks, canals, and waterways where the water crosses the property, perimeter, or community can make it less accessible for attackers.

Before defensive wire was invented, people built wooden palisade walls. This is done by sinking long sharp poles in the ground, side-by-side, until you have a fence. Lashing diagonal and horizontal poles to the fence makes it sturdier. It is a lot of work, but it is easier to go around than over, thus it will channel an enemy.

If you have trees but no wire, you can make timber abatis by sharpening short poles and lashing them in an X-pattern to a center horizontal log or pole. This creates a heavy horizontal obstacle with thousands of sharp points.

Keep in mind to have redundancy and keep improving! If you successfully laid a good triple-strand concertina wire obstacle, now start digging an anti-vehicle ditch or drop a few loads of large rocks to deter trucks from crashing the wire.

Early Warning: This can be as low-tech as soup cans with rocks inside that are hung in the concertina wire, to as high-tech as IR cameras and ground sensors. Whatever your means, do not overlook early warning measures. If the situation is dire enough, a combination of noise devices and booby-traps may be what you need.

Your imagination is the limit really. I have seen noise devices made of everything from tripwires and soda cans to converted alarm buzzers.

The key thing is "early warning". Anyone can walk up to a wire obstacle in the dark and start quietly cutting it down. However, it is another matter if every strand is connected to trip flares or dozens of noisy bundles of bottles and cans hung in the overhead trees.

Overwatch: Even if a defense is not always fully manned, someone should overwatch obstacles. Without overwatch, the obstacles can be breached or bypassed before you even know it has happened.

A wire obstacle is a good example for overwatch. Anyone can build a "wire ramp" by bolting boards to heavy carpet. You throw the ramp over the wire, making the wire sag down, and then people can literally run over the fence. If you are not over watching the obstacle, such a thing can happen.

Primary/Alternate Fighting Positions: Having both primary and alternate fighting positions does two things. First, is assigns sectors of fire, both the main sectors and secondary sectors. This gives you fire control and prevents friendly fire while ensuring every sector is covered. Second, it increases survivability. If you fire several shots from one position, move to fire from the alternate position so no one hones in on your exact location and focuses fires on you.

Primary/Alternate positions can be adjoined or separated. Based on the terrain or structure, you may be able to have both positions just a few feet apart. If they cannot be that close, ensure you have a covered route between both positions. Never put the positions so far apart that you have a substantial lapse in manning either position.

Mutual Supporting Firing Positions: Ideally, every position should be able to be protected by another position. This may not always be 100% possible, but as many positions as possible should be defended from both sides by other positions. Failing to follow this rule may result in your defense being flanked, rolled up, and overran. Try to never leave a position alone and unsupported.

Interlocking Fields of Fire: The use of interlocking fields of fire is one of the most underestimated and misunderstood concepts of a defense. It is a force multiplier that maximizes the mutually supported fighting positions.

When an enemy is deep in the kill zone, none of your fighting positions should engage the enemy from the direct front. The fire should hit him at oblique angles on either side of him (preferably on both sides). Your fires should form X's in the kill zone center. You are shooting the enemy who is in front of the adjacent position beside you; your adjacent buddy next to you is shooting the enemy at your front.

If you are shooting straight into the enemy's direction of travel, the enemy can fire straight back at you as he advances! However, if the fighting positions are arranged (built) so that you shoot the enemy at oblique angles on either side of him, the enemy is only going to shoot dirt if he continues to advance while firing. To accurately return fire at you, the enemy must stop and turn to face you. By stopping, he loses the momentum of his advance and is now a stationary target in the kill zone. If he stops and fires left, he gets hit from his right, and vice versa.

Properly planned interlocking fields of fire will cause a direct assault to dissolve itself. Some of the enemy will advance harmlessly forward until shot at close range, other enemy will stop the assault to fight back but get shot from both sides.

The key is building your positions so your cover is in front of you and everyone fires outward at a roughly 45 degree angle.

<u>Mobile Reserve</u>: A small amount of your force should be dedicated as a mobile reserve. Their job is to reinforce weak places in the defense or strengthen an area that is failing. While defending a loan building or bridge, the reserve may only be one or two men. For

defending a community, this could be many men with several vehicles, etc.

Other helpful things in the defense:

1. A sector sketch of the area, aka Range Card, to ensure everything is covered. Use it during rehearsals too. Making a range card at every position and use that to make a main sector card if you want to be thorough.
2. Actually have someone walk the terrain to let the gunners verify from their positions that they have a field of fire! You may find hidden dead-space and avenues of approach.
3. If the defended area is large, divide it into quadrants. Top right, bottom left, etc.
4. Assign target reference points (TRP's) so that you can quickly communicate where the enemy is in the sector. "TRP 1 is the intersection; TRP 2 is the rock pile; TRP 3 is the abandoned car..."

Something worth discussion here is the **Keyhole Firing Position**. It is often said that people killed in combat never saw what killed them; that for the most part is true. People who have not been shot at before have a strange habit of standing in windows with their barrel hanging out of it, or at the edge of a woodline so they can see better, or at the forward most edge of the alleyway, doorway, etc. Maybe we can blame Hollywood. You do not meet many folks with that habit who have much battle experience, because the ones who did not learn a better way are dead.

If you shoot from the edge of a window or from the forward edge of the trees, how long do you think it will take to catch a bullet? Not long.

A Keyhole is when you fire from so far back that the only enemy that can see you is the one you are shooting. If the other enemies want to know where you shot from, they will have to ask their dead comrade.

In a building you build your position in the back of the room, as far from the window as you can. In a parking lot you find a field of view from several car rows deep. In the woods you stay back in the trees and cover a "hole" between the trees. Sometimes objects like dumpsters give you a keyhole; other times even the terrain may form the keyhole. If you are covering the stair top, you lay on the floor as far back as you can get, and shoot the heads as they appear; to the attackers below, all they can tell is the first guys got shot, and they have zero idea where the fire is from.

Keyhole Firing Positions also allow a hasty "hunter/killer" defense. The hunter takes up a good concealed and covered position with a good field of view; he or she does not fire. The killers take up interlocking fields of fire from keyholes. The hunter calls out the enemy locations based on reference points; the killers take the shots. The enemy looks for the concealed shooters, allowing the hunter to be exposed enough to keep finding targets.

4. Patrolling

What is a patrol? It is a detachment sent from a larger element to perform a specific task. What does a patrol do? A patrol can be doing anything from delivering the mail, to foraging, to checking on a neighbor, but also series of patrols help secure an area and gather intelligence. Keep in mind the 'security and gathering intelligence' because all patrols have that in common anyway. In the days before satellites and UAV's, the only reliable way to gather intelligence was to send a patrol to look and report back.

Anytime you leave a secure area, you ought to treat the movement like a patrol. Some may argue that, "If I'm just driving my people down to the market that is a convoy, not a patrol." That could be true, but if you allow me to split the hairs, I will tell you this: A convoy depends on a separate element to protect it, while a patrol secures itself with security organic to itself. For that reason, I recommend treating all movement like a patrol…whether it is a one man patrol going to deliver a message or 50 people in ten vehicles relocating to a new settlement.

You do not want to be moving around half-cocked and unprepared. Patrolling has principles, and these fundamentals will keep you alive. The principles happen before and during the patrol; some happen simultaneously. The principles apply to patrols that are mounted and/or dismounted. The 5 Principles of Patrolling are: Security; Planning; Reconnaissance; Control; and Common Sense.

Security: Always the most important principle in anything. Security is like gravity; it is constant and if it ever lapses something horrible will happen!

From the very beginning we assign responsibilities for security. Who is on point and who is on trail, who covers the left, who covers the right? What is our speed? What is our dispersion? Who is navigating (I prefer that the point does not have the full burden of navigation, so they are not distracted)? If we stop to rest, how long before we take a knee, get in the prone, or if mounted get off the road? When we halt to rest, are we 100% every man pulling security or 50%, 25% behind a weapon?

In the security plan we talk about and rehearse actions on contact. What if we encounter a booby-trap/IED? How do we react if we have to turn around? What if ambushed? What if we receive small arms fire? Rehearse! Rehearse! Rehearse!

Situational awareness (aka SA) is crucial. People simply do not see what kills them. Looking and seeing are 2 different things. Civilians are trained to "look"…everything from books, webpages, newspapers, magazines, even street signs, are designed to get your eyes to just look at a certain spot. From the earliest days of school, the teacher trained you to look at a certain place on the board etc. The result is that civilians grow up and can "look", but must relearn how to "see".

In the world where anything manmade may kill you and sudden changes in patterns are a bad thing, looking is not good enough. *You must train your eyes to notice changes in shape, changes in colors, and changes in patterns of life.*

One way to train your eyes is to develop a scan technique. Scanning is about using multiple perspectives in a systematic way to search for details. While moving and every time you stop; build a habit of scanning close/near/far for threats. This applies to walking or driving. When your vehicles halt, the first step is to glance under the vehicle in front of and behind you; they also glance under your vehicle (looking for threats like pressure plates, tilt rods, pressure wires). If you are going to get out, you always look down before you step out. Next you scan close (about 5 yards), then scan near (about 25-30 yards), then scan far (depends on terrain; 50-400 yards). Anytime you move, look back and rescan. Scan fast first, then search again more slowly for details.

Planning: We have to cover all the routine stuff; like food, fuel, water, etc. We also must assign duties to individuals. PACE (Chapter 2)

Make sure everyone knows the plan! Not just listens to the plan, but can explain it.

Reconnaissance: Your recon is essential to your planning and should go hand-in-hand. At a minimum, do a map recon, trying to anticipate areas to avoid or potentially good areas to halt. If possible, have someone who is familiar with the route/area/population present.

Note significant terrain in your recon and implement that in planning. Consider that terrain can be a weapon; terrain can limit your mobility as well as an enemy's. Any terrain, even a tiny ditch can stop a bullet. A small hill can hide the maneuver of an army. Terrain works both ways, so make note of it and aggressively use it.

Remember that people are part of the landscape, so include that data in your recon. Are there bandits/militia? Is there a government presence? What is the disposition of the locals and what is their daily routine? Who are important people in the area (mayor/preacher/sheriff/doctor/war lord)?

What are the environmental effects in the area? Are the roads bad? What are the consequences of weather/light/etc?

One of the best ways to memorize an area and to learn about it is to build a terrain model or sand table of the area. This also allows you to more easily brief the mission and do rehearsals, talk-through, and rock drills.

Your recon is ongoing. Before, during, and after the patrol, all the data from your reconnaissance is relevant. Debrief after your patrol and record what you learned for later.

Control: You do not want to be out there in a mob with no one in control. You need people in control at multiple echelons; a senior leader to command, and then a few subordinates to control their subordinates. Ever heard the phrase "command & control"? The officer commands, the NCO's control. It is a great system that works well. The primary leader makes a decision and gives the command, and then his subordinate leaders control all the pieces of making the command become a reality; this allows the primary leader to remain objective and focus on staying ahead of what is happening.

Patrols require control measures, for the most mundane things all the way to extreme circumstances. What is my sector of security? When do I abandon my sector to cover another sector? What are my group's rules of engagement? Can I start my vehicle any time I want, or will we crank up simultaneously (noise disciple)? Can I jump on the radio for _____ or is this worth breaking electronic silence? When do I report my fuel status? When do we move from a file formation to a staggered column?

Common Sense: Ask questions. Make mistakes, admit the mistakes, and learn from the mistakes. Leave your ego in the bedroom and conduct your duties with an open mind.

Listen to advice! I did not say you must *take the advice*, but at least hear the advice.

They say, "common sense is uncommon", and that is mostly true. It is not because people are dumb; on the contrary a person who is not emotional is spectacularly smart most of the time. For simple things 10 people can look at a thing and all 10 people will arrive at 1 or 2 equally correct conclusions. But for more complex things, or unordinary things outside the realm of peoples' usual circumstances, 10 people can look at that thing and arrive at 45 crazy conclusions. After teaching combat patrolling for 3 years as an army instructor, for Army, Navy, Air Force, DoD, and allies, I always thought I had seen it all, but every time the next class would come along and I would see some students make a conclusion even crazier. (Folks assume all military people do patrols, but it is not so. Some will have done over 100 combat patrols in a few months; some will have done a few random patrols over the last several years; but a lot of them can go a full 20 year career and never see a patrol anywhere but on TV.)

Common sense is a thing you learn from doing. A master carpenter will seem like a dummy if you throw him into a surgeon's job, and a surgeon will seem like a dummy if you throw him into a farmer's job, and the best farmer will seem like a dummy if you throw him in an astronaut's job…you get the idea. Well, patrolling is part of soldiering and soldiering is a profession just like a surgeon or astronaut. It takes years to get highly proficient at some things, and then you still learn more every time you do it.

I say all that about common sense to humbly and respectfully submit to you these two things: One, if your group is made of craftsmen, waitresses, cashiers, nurses, and etc or anything of the like…take it very slow! If the world has a catastrophe, do not just go out the next day and patrol the county because you think you can, or go off on a Lewis 'n Clarke expedition. Two, if patrolling is part of your security strategy, do your best to practice and learn it before it is critical.

Keys to success: Teamwork ←
Communication ← Discipline

NOTE: A bit of a warning here and my philosophy on when to patrol: All of us have heard other survivalist explain much of their survival strategies, and patrolling is a very common theme for security, foraging, etc. We hear it from friends, on the internet, in survival circles, and on those cable TV shows. I am not the last word on this, it is only my opinion, but I have worked in disaster areas and want to share my philosophy about *when to patrol* and hope it sinks in.

After most disasters/catastrophes there are a lot of displaced people (aka refugees, in loose use of the legal term). They are either running from the catalyst towards refuge, or having to live on the move to find sustenance, or both. If you have never seen this flood of people, it is astonishing to behold. Places that look like they could not possibly have a large population somehow just fill the roads with crowds and jam-packed vehicles consisting of anything with wheels. The trash is literally knee deep and covers ponds and streams. They will camp anywhere there is room to lay down; often moving much further from the main roads than you would ever expect. I can go on and on, but at risk of you thinking I exaggerate.

Such migration can only go on so long. They will either go where they are going to go or they will settle down where they can sustain, and as they say, that is that. The dust will settle and a new normalcy will begin to occur. In the meantime, if you do not have to go mingle in that flood, why on earth would you, for any conceivable reason, go wander among the flood of humanity? It does not matter if you call it a patrol or walking the dog, what can you possibly do to improve your position by roaming into such a torrent?

When I have asked these questions before, I was told along the lines, "I would patrol in force and gather intelligence from some of the people. They may have relevant news." My experience as a soldier gives me a different view. As a soldier, I had a vast amount of timely information available to me at my fingertips most of the time. And I *never* met a refugee that had the vaguest clue about anything further than the last mile behind him. Rumors among refugees are so powerful, telling them the truth is a pointless exercise that creates a debate that wastes your time.

So you expend manpower, time, and resources to leave your secure area, to get intelligence from someone that will tell you rumors...and your reward is? Your reward most likely could be causing your patrol to get followed home by a horde of desperate people. (Or as my good friend used to say, not people—apex predators.)

Whether the refugee factor is relevant or not, some places like North America have an entirely separate and unique aspect to consider. That is, all the countless people who have armed themselves to the teeth, dressed up in as much tactical gear as they could afford, filled bags full of gadgets and MRE's, built "zombie hunting mobiles", and intend to hit the countryside for who knows what. Some of the folks have military or law enforcement experience; many do not. These fellows are prevalent on the internet; they even make cable TV shows about them!

My intent is not to disrespect these folks. Most probably have decent intentions, however slightly naïve. I am not saying they are bad people. But a lot of them are going to cross paths with other armed people, and out of plain inexperience and simple ignorance more than a few are going to shoot the hell out of each other. Some may just shoot it out because they can.

A look across the open internet survival discussions, blogs, and articles will familiarize you with this common attitude about patrolling, property lines, interacting with other groups, and etc. Some folks are tongue 'n cheek. A lot are very serious. Some have good ideas. Many are misguided. I once listened at a gun show as a young man explained when his group encounters another group, he will order his group to get on line (form a linear line facing another force) behind cover, and then establish communication...*but hold on right there*; jumping behind cover and making a linear formation is a universal maneuver preempting an attack, that will at a minimum escalate tension, or more likely cause the other group to instantly open fire. Anybody with a brain that sees you get in attack formation is going to start shooting.

Do not underestimate the fact that some people intend to shoot first, ask later. I have lost count of how many people over the years I heard say they will shoot strangers or trespassers on sight. (Is that maybe a good reason to be acquainted with the neighbors?)

Then there is the biohazard factor. At best, refugees leave open sewage everywhere that the sun dries up, which turns to dust that blows all around. Healthy well-fed soldiers and aid workers can tell you stories about getting respiratory infections from working near such. At worst, exhausted refugees lose their immune system and begin to host every illness you can think of, which may spread to every healthy human they encounter.

Biohazard can also be the actual disaster. What if you planned to survive global economic collapse, but a super-flu beats the collapse to the punch? Using patrolling in your security strategy takes on new dimensions. Getting shot at may be the least of the problem.

Perhaps (insert a little friendly sarcasm) you have a gigantic group with enormous resources, and if the world falls flat you can swiftly carve out your own miniature country with a new infrastructure, enforce justice, defend your border, create a hospital, envelope refugees into your population and live happily ever after. However, I think most of us will be delighted if we can just safely establish a functioning small farm and institute adequate trade, or some similar lifestyle. I know many people have no further ambition beyond surviving up to about 1 year on their own, and anticipate by then the disaster will be over and things will be back like they were before.

For these reasons and a few more, my philosophy is this: On the question of *when to patrol*, let the dust settle first. Based on the situation, it could be wise to hang as tight as you can for 5 or 10 days, perhaps longer if you could manage. In urban areas this may mean never leaving shouting range from shelter. In rural areas, avoid the main road or waterway, staying well within your property boundaries for awhile, unless you absolutely must check on something. Some folks, depending where you are, may be better off just not patrolling.

I try to prepare to lay very low for 2 weeks to a month. A gunfight is about as much fun as passing a kidney stone. Within 2 weeks to a month, the gun shop warriors and catalog commandos not fertilizing the ditches, or that crippled and maimed each other, will have chosen a more peaceful disposition. And a month of humping a rifle will pacify most of the wannabe-mercenaries that want to stalk the countryside in their "operator" outfit. Once they find out that a daily long-range patrolling routine equals being bug food, smelling like balls, sleeping in soaked clothes, ass rash, blisters the size of tuna cans, insect stings, sunburn, hypothermia, fever, diarrhea, improper sleep, an exhausting level of awareness, maddening boredom, the $200 rucksack they bought is 4 times bigger than they needed and the junk inside is still too heavy, the $200 Gore-tex® boots were not meant for walking anywhere but into a deer blind, being driven crazy by other morons on the patrol…and the thanks for all that work is getting shot at by somebody from somewhere you cannot even see…the wannabe-mercenaries that do not become plant food or rich war lords will find a new line of work, perhaps as exchange laborers in a generous community.

After the gun shop warriors, catalog commandos, and the wannabe-mercenaries have their brief run, I predict it will be safer for the rest of us to begin patrolling to create routes for forging trade relationships and a new barter system. There will still be threats, maybe even worse threats in some regards, but a lot less of them numerically.

Of course you can do anything you like, but just consider waiting to conduct patrols.

5. Vehicle Survival

Even under normal circumstances, carjacking is a real possibility. Criminals use force to steal vehicles from drivers every day around the world. Now think of a situation where fuel and running vehicles are rare commodities and carjacking goes from possible to probable. Large amounts of people who are not necessarily criminals, but become stranded in very desperate circumstances, may do anything to get transportation to escape.

If you have a functioning vehicle of any type during or after a major disaster, whether it is just an ATV or if it is a luxury RV, do not take possession of that machine for granted. Since most people have a car, truck, van, or SUV, this class of vehicle is what we will discuss here. For purpose of this discussion, we are not talking about normal circumstances where emergency services are available and/or you can call your insurance to simply replace the stolen vehicle; let us assume a major catastrophe has unfolded and your daily survival is in peril for the foreseeable future.

Your first line of vehicle defense is your decisions.

1. Only travel for deliberate, well calculated reasons. Do not just run around half-cocked.
2. Use PACE Planning (Chapter 2) and the 5 Principles of Patrolling (Chapter 4).
3. Do not travel alone. If you have the resources, roll in force with multiple vehicles (and towing tackle).
4. Be suspicious of anyone. Example: An easy and effective carjacking tactic is a "Back Door Bob"; several harmless-looking people approach to distract from the passenger side while one gunman moves to the driver door.
5. When in doubt; Move!
6. Use the door locks and seatbelts at all times.
7. Do not rush to failure; speed is not security. Drive at speeds that you can detect threats and react.
8. Always have multiple ways out.
9. Do not pick up strangers.
10. Perform daily maintenance checks.
11. Have a "load plan". Everything in the vehicle should be stowed in a

compartment or strapped down. **Everything** in a vehicle not tied down or locked up will become a dangerous missile in a crash or if you must ram anything.

12. Keep your handguns holstered. (See #11) Even in just a 25mph (40kph) impact, loose pistols, phones, radios, and etc fly all over the passenger cabin. When you need the handgun the most, it could be in the cargo area while you are in the front seat.

Understand that standing your ground to fight in a civilian passenger vehicle is a very bad idea! Two things you really want when bullets fly is *distance* and *ballistic protection.* And civilian passenger vehicle do not have ballistic protection from anything except warm piss. (When my unit had armored SUV's, rated to stop 7.62mm NATO, we found even that was incredibly unsatisfactory against anything but a brief volume of rifle fire.)

First of all, if your goal is to survive, then why stand and fight anyway? If you can quickly drive away (in a fast but controlled manner!), there is nothing to gain from being in a firefight. A civilian passenger vehicle has no ballistic protection, but even if it has 4 flat tires, it can create distance. Drive to safety; drive to a hard structure or something you can defend; drive to somewhere that the terrain puts the enemy at the greatest disadvantage. But do not sit still and die in a flimsy metal box.

Second, you must appreciate just how lacking modern vehicles are in ballistic protection. Since crash safety standards were first introduced decades ago, cars have been made of increasingly more pliable materials that crumple and absorb energy in a crash. Every year cars have more and more plastic instead of metal. Combine that with the push for fuel economy, the frames are made of lightweight alloys that are a very long way from what constitutes "armor" or "armor grade steel/alloy". The pillars in your passenger cabin (A pillar, B pillar, etc) are made to bear weight in a rollover, not to stop a bullet. All this combines to create a vehicle that does not give protection from bullets.

My experience training around scrap cars on ranges, shooting cars and shooting from them, and what I saw in combat zones, is that 9mm, 5.56mm, and 7.62mm, zips completely through civilian vehicles—through the frame, the doors, the glass, the roof, the trunk/cargo/boot. The engine, transmission, some differentials, and the brake disks are about the only things you may count on to halt a bullet.

Many folks have a notion of pulling their handgun and fighting a close-range threat from the driver seat. This is an incredibly poor idea if you can drive away.

Keep in mind that *your car does not stop bullets*. It does have many blind spots however. While you are immobilized in your seat, a threat can easily step in and out of your blind spots...and shoot you through those spots like a fish in a barrel while you vainly search for a target. The closer the threat is, the less lateral distance he must use to move into your blind spots. Remember that a **tactic** is <u>a way to place yourself where you can do the most damage to the enemy and he can do the least damage to you</u>. Trying to fight in an immobilized or stationary car is a tactic that gives the enemy everything and leaves you dead.

If you cannot drive away, grab your rifle/shotgun and exit the car, move to the nearest cover, and then fight back. (If you only have a handgun: Un-holster the handgun with firing hand and unbuckle your seat belt. Driver, as you push the door open, sweep the handgun muzzle up and along the dashboard/steering wheel so you do not shoot yourself in the groin, genitals, or thighs. Passengers point the handgun muzzle up and sweep the cabin roof so you do not shoot yourself or another passenger. Exit the vehicle and seek cover/return fire.)

Avoid using the vehicle you just exited as cover if you have a better choice, like a ditch, power/light pole, concrete object, tree, curb, etc. In Hollywood the actors take cover behind the tail light of their cool SUV. Those actors are not getting shot at though. What do you think a 7.62mm will do to that tail light and the aluminum sheet around it, or the plastic/pliable metal bumper below it? If you are forced to fight around that vehicle is cover, strive to utilize the engine block as cover; try to shoot around it or under it, not over it or you are an easy silhouette target.

Another reason not to have a habit of using your vehicle as cover is it is an instinctive practice to brace against the vehicle to steady your aim. Everybody else that is scrambling out of the vehicle is going to ruin your aim; the vehicle will bounce up/down/left/right the entire time. (This occurrence is also a factor if you remain in the car to lay suppressive fire for your mates to exit the vehicle; hold your weapon a few inches above the door and you will have a little bit steadier aim. As each body unloads, the suspension will move the entire vehicle.)

Using a vehicle to force your way out of a trap is not as straightforward as it may first appear. Once again, blame Hollywood for spreading "reality".

Avoid using the front of your vehicle to ram or push your way past a blocking vehicle. Using the front is likely to damage your radiator and your engine will overheat within several minutes. Depending on your vehicle, striking with the front may fire your airbags. Some vehicles also have a fuel inertia shut-off switch; the switch detects the deceleration of an impact and closes a valve in the fuel line (check your owner's manual).

If you must ram or push your way past a blocking vehicle, try to use the rear of your vehicle. It is greatly less likely to disable your vehicle. Hit the blocking vehicle well under 30mph/50kph, then gun the engine to push it aside. Where do you hit the blocking vehicle? It is best to contact the blocking vehicle as far to the rear as possible. The tail of a vehicle tends to be lighter, thus easier to push away. Also, if the driver has the vehicle in gear, it is most likely in drive/1st gear, and as you approach or when you hit his vehicle he may remove his foot from the brake/clutch and simply roll out of your path.

Consider all this when planning stops. Position your vehicle with multiple escape routes. Plan to use the rear of the vehicle to force your way free if blocked in.

6. Checkpoints/Roadblocks

The way it works is simple: You must pay a "tax" to pass the checkpoint.

An illegal checkpoint (or roadblock) is nothing new in many parts of the world that experience calamity, and the tactic is as old as transportation itself. In many countries everyone from thieves, rogue military/police, militias, to small communities set up checkpoints as a tactic after disasters to increase their wealth, resources, and sometimes political power. Sometimes whatever is passing for a government will post checkpoints in an attempt to seize contraband. Just because it does not happen where you live today does not mean it will not be common down the road from you during/after a large war or massive catastrophe. In the US, there are people who have openly advocated checkpoints as part of a strategy to gather resources after a disaster.

Understand up front that checkpoints are a cheap, low-tech, highly effective tactic for gathering resources. Desperate and wicked people in some places will resort to this tactic to survive.

Checkpoints come in all sizes. It may be just a handful of armed men stopping people walking on a path or from floating down a stream; the men will occasionally move to new areas before too many folks catch on and use another route. Or it could be a large permanent barrier along a highway, or at a sea port, manned by up to a hundred armed men who also perform patrols in the area. Most often checkpoints are mobile though. They will use large vehicles and portable barriers to block the road, sporadically moving and reestablishing the operation; this is called a "snap checkpoint".

They may also use a "non-kinetic ambush". This is when they hide camouflaged off the trail or road and wait for a signal from spotters. When you pass the trigger line, armed men and/or vehicles will move from hide positions onto the trail or road and block you in. The intent is the same as a static checkpoint.

Placement of checkpoints is generally decided by the terrain. Other factors may include remoteness from government or law enforcement, conceal-ability, vulnerability of people in a certain area, volume of travelers or refugees, targeting of certain ethnics or religions, degree of wealth along certain routes, and political disposition.

In the case of terrain, normally they want a bottleneck or choke point; or a place where travel converges to a specific point. Places like mountain passes, bridges, levees, and swamp roads are examples of bottlenecks and choke points. A bottleneck is ideal because it increases the likelihood of you travelling through there, and once you are there the only way out is forwards or backwards. The terrain itself acts as a weapon against you by limiting your maneuverability.

It does them no good if you detect them in time to change directions. Therefore, a checkpoint is placed in a way that once you see it, then it is too late. In open or un-wooded terrain, they place it in the low-ground or on the reverse slope of a hill. In forested places or urban terrain, they place it after a sharp bend in the road or around the corner. On rivers it works the same way.

The reason the threat of checkpoints must be taken seriously is they are pretty common and once at one you may be at the mercy of evil people. Keep in mind, at best the people that man these illegal checkpoints are capitalizing on a disaster by taking possessions from people who are already too poor for security, are displaced and homeless, or are already generally helpless.

Some checkpoints may operate with a relatively nonviolent policy of collecting their tax, based on the fact that you cannot tax a corpse later. However, you cannot count on kindness under such circumstances. Both distant and recent history around the world, on land and water, has proven that atrocities against people are very frequent at such checkpoints. Some people get totally robbed of every possession. Some people get gang raped—and not just women, but men, children, and elderly. Sex slaves are a type of currency, like trading sheep for other commodities. It is not uncommon for ethnic and religious cleansing to occur at checkpoints; if you are the wrong race, color, heritage, or religion you may join a pile in a ditch nearby.

Your very best defense as a traveler is information. Talk to other people when it is safe to do so. Ask travelers headed the opposite way what the path is like. If possible, monitor whatever radio frequencies you have access to. (In the US, on CB channel 17, on any given highway you can hear what mile marker police are sitting at up to an hour before you get there.

It is not uncommon to hear about wrecks or traffic jams hundreds of miles before you arrive.) Just remember if you can monitor the radio, so can the enemy.

Your next line of defense is things we already discussed. Use PACE to plan. Know where you can detour and where bottlenecks are. Do not wait until you are in a disaster or warzone to find an assortment of good maps of where you live, of your retreat areas, or any routes in between. Road maps are fairly helpful. Even better are military topographical (aka topo) maps in 1:25,000 or 1:50,000 scale (try to get maps less than a decade old if possible). Also good are USGS maps; you can find these in topo, aerial, and satellite image. There is also free software on the internet that lets you print or save very recent, highly detailed satellite imagery of anywhere on Earth.

Treat all movement like a patrol. If you are able, move in force, with an element out in front on point. Take your time on the move; speed is not security. Consider your type of vehicles. A big RV is a lot harder to turn around and flee in than a jeep or small SUV.

Change tactics faster than the enemy. Some people may be better off travelling cross-country on foot, horseback, or etc. If local bandits are placing checkpoints on roads, attempt to do your travelling by water, or vice versa.

Can you fight your way out of an illegal checkpoint? Anything is possible. However, a checkpoint is normally designed to put you at a hopeless disadvantage once you are stopped in it. You will be covered in crossfire by armed men behind cover that you cannot shoot. Think of it like a gnat in a spider's web. The gnat's best chance was to use every resource nature gave him to avoid the web.

If you have the resources and support of the local population, capturing and removing men who have ran or are manning illegal checkpoints is probably effort well spent.

7. Going Off-Road

This chapter may not entirely apply to everyone. Some live in urban places and intend to bug-in and other folks already live at their retreat. Others do not plan on using vehicles of any capacity. Yet others will use waterways exclusively.

However, for the person or family who intends to bug-out and travel more than 20 miles (30+ kilometers) to your retreat, a 4x4 off-road vehicle may be a very wise idea. At a minimum, some off-road recovery gear for a 4x2 truck or an SUV could be prudent.

More times than I can count I have heard of a family intending to travel 150+ miles to their retreat in a minivan, 4x2 SUV, or sedan. This always struck me as very odd thinking to spend so much money preparing a very nice retreat, and then plan to get there in a vehicle which is highly dependent on pavement.

A common thought has probably crossed all our minds before: "What if all the roads are jammed?" If you analyze where you plan to go, you will begin to see that with every mile you must travel the probability of a road being impassable exponentially increases. Most of us have saw a major interstate closed a few hours because of a wreck; now imagine it when no one is coming to clean it up, and then multiply that several times due to people panicking during a catastrophe. Things always go wrong in pairs or threes, so factor all that in with bad weather, and then add some darkness. If you think about it, what you may see is yourself stuck halfway between home and your retreat with thousands of other people that cannot leave the obstructed road or highway.

I admit I am a lifelong off-road enthusiast. However, my point is not to try to tell you to buy a 4x4 off-road vehicle, but to make you aware of how vulnerable 4x2 vehicles are. I can tell you 2 easy examples that fully changed my mind about 4x2 street vehicles forever.

The first was after a small ice storm in Texas. I was riding to work and every (I mean every!) stop light had a 4x2 pickup truck trapped that could not move; the lightweight tail ends gave the rear wheels no traction and they were just spinning in place. Some trucks had people stand on the bumpers long enough to get some traction, but at the next light they would just get stuck again.

The second was in Louisiana. My unit was meeting at a small park to do a trail run early in the morning. In our civilian vehicles, we left the road and parked at the bottom of a tiny hill near the trail. We were parked in a small field; freshly mowed well-manicured grass. During the hour we ran the trails, a brief refreshing rain, almost just a drizzle, came and went. When it came time to leave…most vehicles could not get more than 10 feet up the tiny hill. The tires on all the 4x2 vehicles, whether front-wheel drive or rear-wheel drive, were just spinning on the grass. Not even digging in any mud, they just spun like the grass was covered in oil. But it was just damp grass. Luckily, the guys in my unit with 4x4's had nylon tow straps to pull everyone back to the road.

I can give more examples but the point is the same: Be advised that 4x2 vehicles cannot be counted on to leave the pavement. Think of it as survival of the fittest, meaning that some vehicles are less fit than others.

Why would I ever leave the pavement? Maybe power lines are in the road and if you do not go around them off-road you will need to turn back 20 miles to reroute. Perhaps the bridge is blocked or down, and the fastest way upriver to a serviceable bridge is off the concrete. Possibly, if you could leave the highway you can escape a huge traffic jam and get to a detour road across a field. There are countless scenarios where jumping off the pavement for 20 minutes may mean you getting to your retreat (or escaping immediate danger) hours or days sooner. In my humble opinion, having a 4x4 may be the difference in ever reaching your retreat at all.

My bug-out vehicles are a Jeep Wrangler and a Ford 4x4 F150. Both are enhanced somewhat for a little extra off-road ability. It took me years to modify them to what I wanted, but in the end the cost and time was far less than building and stocking a good retreat property. Expensive you may say? I suppose yes, some folks would think so, and some would call it cheap though ($32,000 total to buy 2 pre-owned vehicles and add modifications). However, I shiver at the thought of transporting my family across the chaos of a catastrophe in a sedan or Barbie-style SUV.

The big advantage of the 4x4 is obviously that it is more forgiving in soft ground and typically has good ground clearance. If a 4x4 gets stuck, it is slightly easier to recover it (I know this because at my off-road club we get everything stuck on purpose just to practice recovery). I must point out that any 4x4 should still carry recovery gear and should have a winch with a weight rating 2X the vehicle gross weight; the winch industry usually says 50% over gross vehicle weight (GVW), but going 2X or (100% over) accounts for the weight of supplies and gear, plus the extra stress of pulling uphill. Example: A 3,500lbs winch line could easily snap pulling a 3,000lbs truck up a slight grade. 8,500lbs+ (3,900kg) is usually plenty for a passenger vehicle, but if you go below the 2X rule it is dangerous, so verify your gross weight in the owner manual and estimate you gear weight before you spend money on a winch. If your suspension can bear the extra weight of the biggest winch, then remember "too much winch" is a never spoken phrase around the mud.

If you have a 4x2 truck or SUV and do not intend to get a 4x4, it is easy to make a recovery kit. Assuming you will not mount an electric winch, most farm supply stores sell "come-a-long" style winches (portable winches) that use a leverage bar to let you winch with your muscles. You will also want a tree strap, a tow strap, tow chains, leather gloves, hi-lift jack, shovel, ax, and a tackle block.

No matter if you drive a 4x4 or a 4x2, always ensure you have the right tires for the terrain. Street tires are just dismal off the concrete. I once saw a Chevy with street tires stuck with the tires spinning on an improved forestry road with less than three inches of mud. Use All-Terrain (AT) or mud tires. The AT tires are compromise, being lot quieter on the pavement than mud tires, but still have much more aggressive traction than street tires. In general, AT tires do well in the snow. Mud tires have the most traction, but are surprisingly loud on hard surfaces. Generally, tires that perform will in the mud also do well in the sand.

Caution: A winch and a hi-lift jack can be very dangerous. Read the manual. Learn to use the devices under supervision from an experienced person. Always use a line-dampener with a winch. Never stand in the path of a line break. Wear leather gloves. Keep fingers away from the fairlead. Never put any part of your body under a vehicle lifted by a jack.

Over the years I have found a few good places to buy off-road gear, in no certain order:

- Tractor Supply Company
- Northern Tool + Supply
- Quadratec
- Cabela's

Note: A Hi-Lift Jack® is greatly superior to the tiny bottle or scissor jack that comes with most new vehicles. A hi-lift raises the vehicle much higher and without you ever getting your arm under the vehicle. Not only can one or two hi-lift type jacks raise a vehicle's tire out of a hole, so you can fill the hole, but a hi-lift can be easily converted to winch a vehicle 2 or 3 feet at a time with straps and chains. Just always lift under a solid point (not the body) and be mindful that the jack can tip without warning.

Basic off-road gear for a bug-out vehicle:

- Owner Manual
- Haynes Repair Manual (or Chilton's)
- Extra fluids, filters, belts, and fusses
- Liquid gasket, JB Weld, WD40, and PB Blaster

- Fire extinguisher
- Extra tire and lug wrench
- 4 cans of Fix-a-Flat and a tire repair kit
- Cobra® Power Inverter
- Emergency air compressor
- 2x utility flashlight and extra batteries
- Basic tool kit (ratchet/sockets, wrenches, pliers, screw drivers, Allen wrenches)
- Electrical tape and duct tape
- Bungie cords and 100' of 550 cord
- CB radio
- Basic first aid kit
- 2x leather gloves, with extra wool inserts
- Extra fuel in safety containers
- Hi-Lift Jack® and accessories
- Shovel, ax, machete, and/or E-tool
- Tree strap
- 2" X 20' 20,000lbs recovery straps x 2 and chains
- 18,000lbs snatch block
- Jumper cables
- 6'x8' tarp

- Leatherman or Gerber multi-tool
- Butane lighter x 2 and waterproofed matches
- Solar recharge kit (if travelling solo vehicle)

*List does not include personal items, food, water, weapons, etc.

Not everyone needs an off-road vehicle. All of us have unique requirements based on our unique circumstances and all of us have a different idea about what our emergencies will look like. However, if you know your survival may depend on driving a long distance, I encourage you to look very closely at the route you intend to take and decide if your car can make it if the pavement stops being an option.

8. Waterways

Why limit yourself to the land? Since the beginning of mankind, we have used the waterways to travel and as a source of harvesting food. Before we had invented the wheel or tamed a horse, people had been building rafts and boats for centuries. Over the millennia's we learned to use currents and tides to mechanically power machinery, like mills, and even to create electricity. Being near bodies of water truly can make your life easier and more fruitful. For those reasons I always make an effort to place myself reasonably close to water. As long as you respect the forces of Mother Nature, it is just good survival business.

Being able to get out on the water should always be a strongly contemplated option. Even just a simple canoe can let you flee to places a pursuer may not follow; lets you use a river or lake to reach other communities; and lets you reach new places to fish, string trotlines or yo-yo's, place nets, or run traps. Almost any boat can be loaded up as a "bug-out" boat and then stored for an option in an emergency. If the roads are useless…go to the water and use the boat.

A positive characteristic of boating is it can be accomplished with little or no fuel. You never have to feed a boat and if it has no engine you never have to find any gasoline. If you have some deep-cycle marine batteries and a solar panel and/or wind turbine, you can keep a trolling motor in business indefinitely. A 45lbs thrust trolling motor can move a canoe or small boat around a lake, canal, swamp, or a slow river very well. For that matter, new boaters are usually surprised how easily and quickly a pair of paddles can move a canoe or johnboat.

A lightweight boat like a canoe or johnboat can also be used to build a hasty lean-to style shelter simply by lashing the boat to a tree or other object. When combined with a tarp or ponchos this makes a reasonably sturdy shelter in a pinch. I have used this trick several times when surprised by unexpected storms.

Some folks will find it harder to incorporate using waterways into their survival strategy than others. If you have not built a retreat yet, consider the advantages of the water in your site selection. Also factor in any history of flooding, surges, or hurricanes. You do not necessarily have to have a beach or riverbank as your backyard; but you want to be reasonably close to the water. An ideal retreat location is on high ground above the flood zone (if applicable), and close enough to freely access the water without excessive effort.

On the other hand, there are people with outstanding access to water and their entire survival strategy revolves around the water. I have met a survivalist with a houseboat on a 50,000 acre lake. While such a setup may not be possible for everyone, it illustrates how large the waterway survival concept can really be.

Whether you plan to place a retreat by the water or not, at a minimum, research the wetlands and waterway access near your area and/or your retreat area. Find out what the wildlife and plant life are. Many plants near water have medical uses (examples: willows and cattails). Inquire if there has been any contamination, like heavy metals. What are the seasonal water levels? Does the water freeze over? Are the lakes or waterways natural or manmade? Who else already uses the water?

Some advantages of being near waterways:

- Water can act as a natural border defense

- Access to fish, plants, and wildlife
- Access to abundant water
- Access to highly fertile mud/soil
- Entry to alternate transportation
- Access to places not reachable by road
- Waterwheels or hydro-generators can be built

Boat selection is important. You would not want to get a 16-foot boat with a trailer if you do not have any boat ramps within practical distance. You do not want a powerboat if you cannot get fuel later. At the same time, you would not want a tiny craft unrated for the sea if you are going to be in saltwater.

The following is a list of three basic boat styles that are easy to use and commonly sold around the world. These boats can run in shallow water:

Kayak: A kayak is a very slender boat built for usually one person, or rarely sometimes two. The advantage is it is very portable and easy to use. Even a 12-foot kayak can weight under 50 lbs (23 kg). A kayak is manpowered; the longer it is the faster it will go. Being so slender and light, it is easy to carry into the woods to hide. The disadvantage is it is relatively unstable and cannot carry hardly any cargo. Prices for polymer models run from $300-$1,000 USD.

Canoe: These highly versatile crafts vary in size (too many to name here), with the smallest able to carry two or three people and the largest carrying many more. Most have a pointed bow and stern, however some have a flat stern meant for a trolling motor or small outboard engine. A canoe is easily propelled by paddles under most conditions. The bottom may be round or flat. The main advantage of a canoe is it is small enough to be easily transported, sleek enough to be maneuvered by paddles, but large enough to carry some cargo. The disadvantage is that a canoe is somewhat unstable and inexperienced or inattentive people may capsize it.

Modern canoes are mainly made of polymer, aluminum, or fiberglass. Most weight less than 100 lbs (45 kg). You can buy wood canoes, but they are heavy and expensive. A canoe will cost from $300-2,000 USD.

Johnboat: (aka jon boat) These boats are typically rectangular in shape and have a flat bottom; they come in various lengths from 8-foot on up to over 20-foot. Most are made of aluminum or fiberglass; some are plastic. These boats are a bit heavy to transport on foot unless you have several people to carry it, but are easy to transport by vehicle either in a truck bed, in a trailer, or even over an SUV roof. They are normally meant to be powered by motor, but using paddles is also realistic under normal conditions. The advantage of a johnboat is its flat bottom makes it stable and it can carry plenty of cargo. The disadvantage is its shape makes it cumbersome to maneuver without a motor on anything but calm water. Price may vary from a few hundred to a few thousand dollars.

Basic gear for a bug-out boat:

- Motor owner's manual/repair manual (if applicable)
- Extra battery or fuel (if applicable)
- Life vest (per person)
- Paddle, full size (per person)
- 50' nylon rope
- 6'x8' tarp x 2
- 2x utility flashlight and extra batteries

- Butane lighter x 2 and waterproofed matches
- Bait net, trotlines with hooks, automatic yo-yo's
- Roll of 16GA bailing wire & steel traps
- Fishing tackle (hooks, sinkers, line, etc)
- Pliers, wire cutters, utility knife, and machete
- First aid kit
- Solar battery charger (if applicable)
- Emergency radio
- Leather gloves with extra wool liners
- Bug repellent, bandanas, and extra hat & sunglasses
- Box of 30 gallon trash bags
- Bungie cords
- 1 gallon metal pot
- 2 quart canteen

*List does not include personal items, food, water, weapons, etc.

On a last note, I have come to think of waterways as more than just an escape or transportation route; more than just a road. The water is an extra garden, another pasture, and an additional forest. You can set your trotlines, automatic fishing yo-yos, and fish or crab traps, and then go about your other business while the fish do the work for you.

The water around the planet is teaming with furbearers. Beaver, mink, muskrat, otter, raccoon, and nutria are just the few of many species that can be trapped near streams, lakes, and rivers. That is a lot of fur and meat that should not be overlooked in a post-apocalypse aftermath.

9. Moving on Foot

"We live in a world of illusions." Joel Skousen

At some point we may need to move an extended distance on foot. Depending on the disaster, moving on foot may be the only option. Either vehicles may not work or the roadways may be hopelessly useless for vehicle traffic. During the period after a disaster, an extended time without fresh fuel will mean almost no vehicles are rolling. Petroleum is perishable.

It is only practical to assume that at some point we will be required to walk.

One thing we need to clearly acknowledge is exactly how far we can realistically walk in an hour, in a day, in a week. There are a lot of deadly incorrect assumptions about this. On the internet and in some books you will read notions that are mortally flawed. I have read the simplified logic of 4mph x 24 hrs = 96 miles in a day. But that uninformed logic absolutely disregards every factor that comes into the biomechanics of walking. Almost any human that really tried to walk 96 miles in a day would end up crippled.

A terrible mistake that people make who have never been forced to walk long distances is that they rarely factor in that you must still be effective and capable on the other end of the walk. So what if I walk 25 miles at a forced pace, just too arrive on the other side so weak that I cannot protect myself? Or if I walk until exhausted, and make myself prone to orthopedic injury? There is a point where you become so tired that your muscles stop performing their secondary role as shock absorption and you start to jar your bones until you get stress fractures and frayed tendons. If you walk beyond the ability of your muscles you will get injured in ways that take a long time to fix. I am a career infantryman; ask me how I know these things.

First, there is the physical side. How far can you literally walk if all else is equal? Second, is how far you can walk on available water and food? Third, is how far will your gear get you and what is its weight? Finally, there are the security factors. How far can you walk without putting yourself at unnecessary security risks?

A very deadly and popular misconception people have sounds like this: "The human body was made to walk 25 miles (40k) in a day" or "A healthy person can walk 20 miles (32k) in a day" or "The human body was made to run 50 miles (80k) in a day". Those people like to point out that Paleolithic man ran their prey to death or Native Americans were known to travel 50 miles a day. Yes, they really did that. Yeah, the human body was *designed* to do that. But if you do not train and condition regularly to do that, you are in for a very agonizing lesson!

It does not matter if you spend 12 hours a day on your feet for 6 days every week; you are not conditioned to walk that far. It does not matter if you walk 2 miles a day...or 6 miles a day, you are not conditioned to walk 25 miles in a day. I learned this as a US Army drill sergeant serving for 3 years. I trained a lot of people. I learned firsthand that high school athletes who can run 1 mile (1.6k) in under 6 minutes, but never trained to run 2 miles, would miserably fail in that second mile. If you train for 10 miles that is what you have. When push comes to shove, you will not magically rise to the occasion; you will be ok for 10 miles. After that you will start to fall off fast.

Eugene Randall

If you train for nothing, you cannot expect to go very far very fast. That is a fact. I tell you that sincerely because you are paying to hear the truth. You will do exactly what you conditioned to do. If you conditioned to do nothing, you will not do much more than that. Paleolithic man really could run a deer to death, but when was the last time you did that?

What my time as a drill sergeant taught me, when transforming civilians into Soldiers, was that your average unconditioned civilian is good for about 4-6 miles (6-10k) of forced walking, or perhaps 10 miles (17k) total in a day, and still be reasonably able to function. It was a fact that anything more than that would typically break a civilian, leaving him ineffective for further training, even if he was a football athlete who just graduated high school. After 4-6 weeks of training was a different story. A young body supported with food delivered daily from trucks conditions remarkably fast. But we are not talking about a place where you will get any support. We are talking about a place where you will be on your own.

So the answer to how far you can literally walk if all else is equal is however far you have been training to walk. If you have not been doing any conditioning whatsoever then less than 10 miles a day is a realistic answer. A forced march speed is 4mph, but it is faster than it sounds if you are not accustomed to that speed. If you have not been training, about 2-3mph is a more reasonable speed. In a week, you are looking at 50-70 miles; and you are going to be very sore.

For every hour you walk, your body will use roughly 1/2 to 1 quart (1 liter) of water. (Never drink more than 1.5 quarts of water per hour.) Your body temperature is going to rise and you are going to sweat a lot; even if it is below freezing, in about 6-8 miles you will sweat completely through your clothing. A big mistake new walkers make is to begin walking in the cold with too much clothing on. You need to strip down to one layer before you walk, or else you may overheat (this reason is why I have witnessed as many heat strokes in the winter time as I have in summer). Then when you get to your destination you will have warm, dry clothes to put on once you begin to cool off, which you will rapidly because you are covered in sweat.

It cannot be emphasized enough how much water you will use. When I was in a unit that foot marched when it was so cold that

Camelbaks would freeze and pop on the march, in less than 10 miles I would still sweat completely through my belt and my boot uppers.

So you must replace your water. Hot or cold does not matter; your body uses water when you walk. Skipping that 1 quart of water for just one hour can reduce your stamina by 25%. Experienced athletes can tell you that it is wise to begin extra hydration at least 12 hours prior too. If you get dehydrated, 5 hours of rest is the minimal time to catch back up. You must have a plan to carry and replace water. A portable water filter system may be a good idea.

Food is also important. The calories are really not what your concern is with. You only burn 100 calories per mile, which is easily replaced. The salt and minerals in the meal is what you need most. Sweating causes you to lose salt. And your body requires salt to metabolize your water. If your body gets low on salt, you end up with heat stroke. If you ever hear a Soldier say, "hydration through meals", that is what he is talking about. Essentially, putting water in a body without food can be deadly. When you stop to rest, include a meal in the break.

How does gear matter? The most merciless enemy you have is gravity. She never rests, she never sleeps; she is a constant that effects everyone. The more junk you carry, the slower you will go.

A good weight for your bag is 35 lbs or less, not including your water. 35 lbs is a manageable weight and allows you to bring a decent amount of items. Once you go over 35 lbs, every ounce will really start to make a difference. I would strive to make my bag as light as possible. The difference between just 45 lbs and 35 lbs could be 2 or 3 miles per day, especially on uneven or hilly terrain. Your water weights 8 lbs per gallon or 1 kilo per liter. And walking 4mph, a gallon does not last long.

Your footwear is crucial. You want walking shoes or boots to fit tight. This reduces part of the friction that causes blisters. Every time you step down, your feet expand under the weight, and when you step up, your feet shrink back to normal size. This action repeated thousands of times over a few miles creates so much heat it literally burns your skin until it blisters. These blisters pop, and then over the next distance you get friction directly to the meat under the skin. It ends up being a painful bloody mess and can incapacitate you from walking. So wear tight footgear to reduce this. And for Heaven's sake, break in the boots before you go on a long walk!

If you are not carrying a bag or extra weight, then running or walking shoes are not a bad idea. But if you are carrying a bag, this type of shoe is pretty poor. They are not made to support the extra weight and they will not. Shoes may feel stable, but once you add a bag and rough ground you get rolled ankles or stress fractures. Obviously if you are going cross-country, these shoes will not serve you well for that either. The cushion in running shoes has a lifespan. I replace mine every 500 miles, because after that the cushion is spent. Keep that in mind for your bug-out shoes, set aside a new broken-in pair for your anticipated trek. Be aware that shoes leave your ankles exposed to critters.

In general, good hiking boots are your best bet. They work well on a variety of surfaces and are made to hold up to lots of walking. They are made to support your body plus the weight of a heavy bag. When worn properly they reduce ankle rolling. Modern hiking boots can be surprisingly lightweight.

They offer some defense from biting insects, thorns, etc.

Military and hunting boots have a lot of merits too. They are tough, durable, and made for the outdoors. They offer the most protection from insects, snakes, and poison plants. The worst mistake you can make is to walk long distance in winterized hunting or military boots. These are simply insulated boots; usually with something like Gortex or Thinsulate. It does not matter if you are in nearly arctic conditions; do not go walk 10+ miles in these boots. This type of boot is made for sitting still in the cold, not for a lot of walking. Your feet are already going to sweat a lot anyway, but now you have added in two factors. One, the insulation traps the sweat and the boots just get heavier. Two, the extra sweat reduces the protection your socks give you from friction while the insulation speeds up the heating process that creates the blisters. Over enough distance and enough time, insulated boots will destroy your feet and leave you unable to go on. For walking, unless it is the type of environment to use a dog sled and snow shoes, get the plain old summer boots (aka hot weather boots)…if you get cold after you stop put on your fresh dry heavyweight socks.

Nike, Rocky, Oakley, and Under Armour all make incredibly comfortable, lightweight, durable military boots.

Bates, Belleville, Danner, and Altama also make very good boots, but aim for their high-end boots for the most comfort; their lower-end boots are basic issue military items and is not that comfortable.

Avoid cheaply made boots. If you find a pair of $30 jungle boots, do not even think about it; they will fall apart right after the tear up your feet. You would be better off putting that $30 towards some used surplus boots.

A good pair of spandex or bicycle shorts under your pants will keep you walking too. Do not wear cotton briefs, boxers, 'tighty-whities', etc because these types of underwear swell up as they soak in your sweat, and around miles 8 or 9 you will feel a funny tingle between your thighs. When you stop, it will be very painful and each step you take will feel like a cigarette burning you. That is because you are raw, and the skin has worn away between your thighs, under your scrotum, and between the crack of your buttocks. Soldiers call this phenomenon "monkey butt" and it is pretty painful. If you are not a lean person, but have a few extra pounds of fat, you will develop the "monkey butt" symptoms faster than a skinny body. Like I said, the way to solve this is to wear spandex or bicycle shorts. I go an extra step and liberally dust my shorts with foot powder for extra friction protection.

Have good socks. I can tell you that a $200 pair of boots will not feel like $200 boots after a few miles wearing $2 socks! Paying for good socks is just as vital as buying quality boots. Save the cotton socks for something besides long distance walking (they are not that bad for recovery after walking actually, if dry) because the cotton loses all friction protection with the slightest moisture and because damp cotton readily breeds bacteria and fungus. Buy real boot socks made of poly-wool blend with thick cushion soles. Carry at least 2 pair of socks per day you plan to walk. Lots of foot powder will extend how long your socks protect your feet. I can recommend Under Armour and Wigwam for seasonal boot socks that work very good.

What about survivability? If you do a forced walk 12 miles straight through in 3 hours, how aware do you think you can actually be of your surroundings? Remember that speed is not security. You do not want to rush into anything you cannot escape.

Let's say you are a few hours or couple days into a major catastrophe. You anticipate that people are going to begin looting and robbing, if in fact they are not already. You have roughly 15 miles to get home and vehicles are not an option. Can you just walk that straight through and be home in about 4 hours? Maybe, but my answer is you should not try.

For security reasons, I advise you to plan yourself 24-48 hours to cover that 15 miles. You will not help anybody by getting yourself killed and you will not help anybody if you arrive unable to do anything but lay down. When we normally think of going home we anticipate resting, hot showers, warm food, safety, and etc. But think about this: If that is true then you are not in any kind of emergency or catastrophe. We have to accept the reality that getting home may be just another chapter in an ongoing relentless nightmare. We have to make it home but also be able to continue through the next crisis, and the next.

What I suggest goes something like this: Start planning now. Already plan out the places you may be forced to walk to and from. Recon the routes and preplan your rest areas. Identify and note terrain features at each mile or kilometer along the route, so you can calculate your speed/progress. Identify bottlenecks like bridges that you may be forced to bypass (or traverse at night). Consider placing small supply caches along the routes; this can greatly reduce the load you need to carry.

Do not attempt to walk the whole distance at once. Start slow and take your time. Walking a slow to moderate pace means you will see and hear more than you will while speed walking. Identify threats early enough to avoid them.

Make a rest cycle. Walk for 30 minutes and then rest out of sight for 15 minutes. This keeps you strong and allows you to watch your back trail for threats. Every 4 or 5 miles, stop for a meal, change socks, use foot powder, and elevate your feet on your bag for a few minutes. After 7 or 8 miles, get some sleep and start back out before dawn; cover a mile or two before the rest of the world wakes up.

The goal is to cover ground but remain strong to deal with any situation. When you get tired you make stupid decisions; do not get tired. You cannot count on adrenaline either. Adrenaline just lets you use the energy you have at an accelerated rate; if you are exhausted, a dose of adrenaline is like stomping the gas pedal on a car running on fumes. Do not think in terms of just going Point A to Point B, plan a few steps ahead.

10. Survival Knives

What images come to mind at the mention of "survival knives"? Most likely a big shiny Rambo-style knife with a hollow handle full of doohickeys and a blade bristling with aggressive saw teeth. Or maybe some exotic tacti-kool knife with a camouflage painted blade comes to thought.

In reality, the true survival knife may look quite plain. After all, it is nothing other than a high-quality knife of such durable and simple design that it will not fail during prolonged usage under severe conditions. Survival knives come in countless shapes, styles, and sizes. What separates it from other knives, thus defines the type of knife, is that it will keep working efficiently when other knives become ineffective during a period when a person has no effort or time to waste on things that will not function. You are not paying for how the knife looks; you are paying for how long it will function acceptably without maintenance.

That type of quality and superiority does cost extra money, but your knives truly are one of those pieces of equipment that you should not skimp on. I have never stopped being amused by individuals who shoot premium ammunition from $1,000 weapons, but balk at owning at least one blade worth $100. If you have ever killed a large animal and had to quarter it in the dark, in subfreezing weather while blood froze to your throbbing fingers, with knives that became too dull before the job was complete, then you know the painful frustration that inspires you to buy a worthy blade.

What do you do when you are exhausted, it is dark and freezing, you are soaked to the skin, you cannot stop to sharpen your knives, when you cannot afford to leave the meat to the coyotes, and there is nowhere nearby to get warm? Or name the scenario, they are infinite. I am not talking about during a recreational camping trip, but when everything has gone wrong and you are on your own. Please hear my humble and respectful advice: If you do not bring tools worthy of the task to Mother Nature, eventually she will kill you without any ceremony or fanfare, and dissolve you and your gear back into the earth from which you came.

Safety: Knives are inherently dangerous and a mistake can leave you helpless.

1. Sharp knives are safer; dull knives do not perform well, thus are dangerous.

2. Never cut toward yourself; this includes sharpening or cleaning.

3. Never cut while distracted.

4. Never use a blade as a pry bar.

5. Never try to catch a falling knife. Just move away.

6. Use the right knife for the right job. This includes not throwing regular knives.

There are two fundamental things that every survivalist should understand about their choices in knives:

1. For every million times your knife is going to be used for mundane ordinary chores will the knife have even the slightest single chance of being needed as a weapon. That is not to say you will absolutely never need to use the knife to protect yourself; it is just to say be

realistic about why you are really going to need the knife. Knives that are purposely built exclusively for fighting tend to be dismal performers during ordinary tasks and dangerous as utility knives; however, a quality utility knife excels at chores and can almost always suffice as a satisfactory weapon.

2. Everyone has a favorite "all-purpose" or "general-purpose" knife…that faithful hunting or camping knife we always rely on. Nonetheless, when you spend enough time outdoors it becomes obvious that one perfect knife is a myth and that you are better off having a few special-purpose knives to compliment that all-purpose knife. Have you ever seen a toolbox contain just one tool? No, because something that is okay at everything is also rarely great at any one thing.

Folder vs. Fixed: The folding knife, just like the handgun, really only exists because of the need for portability. Just like carrying a handgun instead of a rifle, you are really only carrying a folding knife as a compromise to save space or the need for conceal-ability. If you wanted the most efficient and strongest tool, you would never trade a puny handgun for a rifle. The same is true with folding knives. No handgun can reach out with the power of a rifle and no folding knife will safely withstand the workload that a quality fixed blade knife will withstand. It is just simple physics that the folder has a significant point-of-failure that does not exist on a fixed blade. Combine that fact with the reality that folders are built to be more lightweight (i.e. portable) than fixed blades, and you can appreciate that the folder is an inherently weaker design (if not only in design, then in literal product execution).

Does that mean folding knives are worthless? Absolutely not! People carry a handgun *and a rifle* all the time, right? Think of the folding knife the same way. One design compliments the other. Sometimes the conditions call for the smaller design. Sometimes portability or concealment is the biggest factors of practicality. And ultimately you need more than one knife, but space can be limited.

Just do not have any illusions about a folding knife having the strength of a fixed blade knife. Utilize both to fill your needs, but know the limitations of each. Note of caution: When you buy folding knives, do yourself a favor and insist on ones that lock open!

Blade Length/Size: If you study the evolution of firearms, you will also observe that as firearms became increasingly efficient the blades of military and sporting knives steadily decreased in size. This fact is largely due to the fact that the role of blades as weapons exponentially decreased as firearms evolved from single-shot weapons into high-capacity weapons.

The shrinking of the military and sporting blade was also due to marketing and economic reasons. If you study knives from the bronze-age all the way until WW2, you will notice that generally military and sporting knives were remarkably large. But what happened around WW2? When the war ended, most of the modern world found a big market in outdoors recreation. Knives were as big of a business as fishing poles and golf clubs. Why pay for the materials to manufacture big blades if you could convince consumers to pay the same price for knives half the size? It was just good business to make a bigger profit. So the knife manufacturers and outdoor outfitters collaborated on a successful marketing/advertisement campaign to persuade upcoming outdoorsmen that only "tenderfoots, greenhorns, and novices" carried large knives in the wilderness. This sentiment is still around too.

What does this mean for the survivalist? It means this: Yes you do need some small knives in your inventory for tasks that require finesse or delicacy. You need relatively medium knives for everyday ordinary cutting tasks. But it also means you should not hesitate to have a very large knife if you think you need it. Having a big knife does not make you a novice; it means you analyzed your requirements and recognized that a hefty blade is sometimes required.

Small, thin, very sharp blades around 2-3" (5-8cm) tend to be good for delicate tasks like dressing birds, whittling deadfall triggers, and etc. The small blade is easy to control. This is where the folding knife excels, if it has an ergonomic handle. Precise cutting tends to be low stress on the entire knife, with most of the pressure being applied along the edge, and not to the tang.

Medium blades of 4-7" (10-18cm) are apt for general-purpose utility knives. This length is still relatively easy to control for most cutting, but there is enough blade to offer plenty of cutting edge to complete the job. A compromise length, around 5" (12.5cm) is almost perfect for skinning and quartering game. A utility knife may end up doing everything from sharpening stakes, striking flint for fire, cutting rope, carving wood, splitting limbs, to butchering animals. Since you never really know how hard you may end up abusing a utility knife, I greatly recommend you try to have a fixed blade utility knife with an ample tang.

Large blades that are 8-14" (20-35cm) are intended for chores that medium knives cannot tackle. Large blades can be used for most cutting jobs, if no finesse is required, but can also effectively chop. You would not want to skin an animal with a large knife unless you had to because it is slower and more awkward than a medium blade, causing you to expend more effort, but on the other hand the large knife is superior for butchering. The large knife is efficient at chopping and hacking through material that lesser knives cannot handle. In an emergency, knives this size are formidable weapons too.

As a soldier and hunter, time and experience taught me to carry a 3" locking folder, 5" fixed, and 10" fixed blade on my person or kit at all times. Each length is very good for certain tasks, but if one knife is lost or broken, one of the others can perform reasonably close.

Blade Shape: There is no perfect shape and how shape influences performance is mostly subjective. One person may like a fine or acute point on a skinning knife while another person likes an obtuse or swept point. Then yet another person will not perceive any difference in most blade styles, if all else is equal.

In general, it can be agreed that tanto-style blades are best when piercing is a requirement, while a bowie-style blade is better when skinning/slicing/slashing is desired, and Gurkha (kukri) type blades are unsurpassed for chopping. I can tell you that tonto blades are poor for skinning and Gurkha blades behave unpredictably at thrusting/piercing.

Blades with an upward sweep near the tip tend to reign as skinning knives, as the curve creates more cutting surface than a straight knife. A clip-point blade is often preferred for skinning also. Drop-point blades can serve as skinners, but really excel with woodwork, where the larger point lends more strength. Knives with a completely straight back also allow more control when force is applied to the edge.

My advice is two things. First, try a few styles and establish what you like. A glance in a knife catalog and I can identify a dozen different major blade styles, and only you can finally say which are best for you. Do not just guess; try it out and see and you may be surprised. Second, try to generally predict how and where you will need your knives. In an urban area, there are many legitimate reasons to carry a tanto blade, because you will often encounter construction and building materials. However, in a wilderness area, you will need to look really hard to find a valid reason to need a tanto blade. When in doubt, a good compromise anywhere is the bowie-style or clip-point.

Serrations: The short answer is, yes. My advice is to have at least one serrated blade handy. I cannot advise serrations on a skinning blade, but you may find a different preference. For myself, I either get a 1/3 serrated blade, or better yet select a blade with a serrated portion along the spine (back edge) of the blade. A good example is made by KA-BAR, sold as the Big Brother. Other examples are made by Ontario Knife Company.

Steel: It should be understood that steel is not one substance. It is a mixture of many elements, and when the combination of the mixture is changed it creates different types of steel with varying characteristics. Changing the mix by just 0.1% (not 1%, but 0.1%) can create a new type of steel. Also understand that you cannot make a mix with greater than a total of 100%...what I mean is that adding an element that gives one characteristic thus must subtract from other elements in the steel that give other characteristics.

Good survival knife steel, once properly heat treated, is hard enough to hold an edge, but tough and resilient enough to absorb impact or flex without breaking. This combination is not easy to make. Steel that is too hard gets brittle; steel that is too tough or resilient will be too soft to hold an edge. Steel that resists rusting will often not be very hard or be very tough. The perfect combination requires masterful execution in metallurgy...then it requires a master of heat treatment to take it to the furnace.

You can generally divide knife steel into two main categories: Stainless and carbon.

Stainless steel is created by adding 11% or more chromium to the total content. This creates steel that is highly resistant to rusting and corrosion. If you are working in salt water or leave a blade lying wet, this can be desirable protection. However, adding chromium means that other elements in the mix decrease; some of those elements are things which make the steal resilient to abrasion, wear, and shock.

Generally, stainless steel is not as hard or as strong as carbon steel. Stainless steel loses its edge faster and can break under stress or shock easier. There is a big reason real swords are never made of stainless steel—*it will shatter on impact*! Avoid stainless steel in blades over 8" (20cm) because they are prone to breaking. Stainless steel is normally unsuitable for striking real flint.

Why did I say generally? Steel type is important, but heat treatment is paramount. Mediocre steel can be properly heat treated into a good blade, but even the best steel with a bad heat treating makes a substandard blade. For that reason, buy from manufacturers with a good reputation.

There are too many exotic steels to review here, but one that may come to mind is Damascus steel. Some people are convinced this steel is great; that it is very strong and has extra cutting ability. It is simply made by folding any normal steel many times. Is it really stronger? Not at all, because the folds can hide severe faults or weakness that will make the blade catastrophically fail under stress. I think the belief that Damascus steel cuts better came from the myths surrounding Samaria swords' famous cutting ability. The truth is that the Japanese did not fold the sword steel because it gave extra cutting power; *they had to fold their steel* because the Japanese did not have access to quality iron, thus they folded the steel to compensate. It is a fact that genuine Samaria swords are no stronger or sharper than blades that come off production lines today at reputable knife factories.

I do my utmost to only use carbon steel for all my fixed blades; only accepting stainless for small folding knives. Carbon steel easily rusts, and requires constant maintenance and protection (oil) after exposure to moisture. But it is tough, durable, resilient, and easy to sharpen, which to me are qualities that are worth the extra attention. A properly heat treated carbon steel knife will shrug off abuse or absorb impacts that will make a stainless blade fail.

Common knife steel types at a glance (Not comprehensive):

410- Stainless steel used to make everything from springs, to dental tools, to shotgun steel shot, to water valves; also used in low-end import knives.

420- Stainless steel best used in diving knives. It is soft, but will not easily rust. Since it is inexpensive to make, it is found in a lot of budget knives.

420J2- This is another stainless steel you find in very low-priced knives. Some popular knife companies like Kershaw occasionally sell knives made of this cheap steel.

420HC- This stainless steel is one with a bit more carbon in it. It is a bit harder than 420 and still stainless. You can find this steel in most Buck brand knives.

440A- This stainless steel is soft, but resists rust. You can find it in many Kershaw blades. It is okay for light duty. It dulls pretty fast. I used to use this steel for my "swimming knives" because it has better edge retention than 420, but resists corrosion well in brine backwater or salty seawater.

440C- This stainless steel has a high amount of carbon for stainless. Can be tempered pretty hard and it works well in short knives. It will take a sharp edge, but dulls noticeably faster than high carbon steel blades. If you insist on a stainless blade, this steel is sort of the benchmark most other stainless steels are compared to.

AUS-6 (A6) Stainless steel almost identical to 440A, but developed in Japan.

AUS-8 (A8, 440B) Falls between 440A and 440C. You may find a sample in SOG knives.

AUS-10 (A8) Very comparable to 440C.

154CM- (CPM154) This stainless steel is comparable to 440C, but is tougher and slightly harder. It holds a decent edge and can be considered an upgrade over 440C.

ATS-34- This steel is almost identical to 145CM.

N680- This steel is almost identical to 145CM.

13C26- A stainless steel with decent hardness, but it does rust. Kershaw used this steel to replace 440A in some models. It is harder than 440A thus holds an okay edge, but not fantastic.

12C27- Very similar to 13C26.

14C28N- Kershaw used this stainless steel to upgrade their 13C26 blades; it is similar hardness but more resistant to rust.

S30V- (CPM S30V) A fairly high-end stainless steel with good general characteristics.

S60V- (T440V) Another higher-end stainless steel. Boker is probably the only knife manufacturer still using it. Some older, out of production Spyderco's are made of this.

4034- This is a new name for 420 stainless steel.

5CR13- This is an imported steel that is very similar to 440A.

7Cr17Mov- This is another imported steel that is very similar to 440A.

8Cr13MoV- This is an imported steel that is very similar to 440B or AUS-8.

9Cr18MoV- Imported steel very similar to 440C.

D2- This steel started as tool steel, and technically is a type of stainless steel. Its characteristics fall between 440C stainless steel and 1065 carbon steel, thus it is a compromise or hybrid of both extremes, and therefore earned the attention of the knife market. Since this steel was created for impact tools, it is pretty hard to sharpen, and ironically in knife applications it may break easier than 1084 or 1095 blades.

SK-5- A modern Japanese version of 1080 steel that makes a tough blade with a hard edge.

1045- This is a carbon steel. Because it has low carbon content (the 10 is the steel type and the 45 represents the carbon amount per mass), it is comparatively softer than other carbon steels, but it is strong steel when properly heat treated. It will get dull pretty quick and rust easily too. (1055 is comparable but a bit harder.)

1060- This carbon steel is what swords are made of. It is very strong and will flex, thus hard to break. It holds a decent edge, but watch for rust.

1070- This carbon steel is used in large knives and machetes, where a lot of extra flexibility is not necessary, but edge retention is a priority. This steel is hard but can still bend and absorb shock without damage.

1080- (1077, 1084) This is high carbon steel. It has a minor amount of flex, but is made for its ability to hold a good edge. This serves very good for big knives.

1095- This is very high carbon steel. You have to search hard to find very expensive stainless steel to compete with 1095 carbon steel, which is ironic because less than a century ago almost all outdoorsmen carried knives of all sizes made of plain old 1095. It has a tiny amount of flex, absorbs shock well, and has an extremely hard edge, yet it sharpens easily. Just dry it off after you use it because it will certainly rust. (This is my personal favorite choice in steel for survival blades.)

5160- This is a spring steel with the same carbon content as 1060. If you have ever had the pleasure of using a handmade knife made from an old truck spring, this steel is the commercial equivalent. Genuine Gurkha knives are made of this steel class. For very large knives it is almost unequalled.

The bottom line is this: Get the best knives you can afford. If you can meet the expense of paying a custom knife maker to forge the exact knives for your specific goals, then by all means do so, because during a disaster you cannot go back to the store and buy a knife as an afterthought. If you are like most folks and must buy or order knives off the shelf, you are still okay. Just understand that commercial knife manufacturers have to balance selling you a decent knife with making a profit to stay in business. You have to balance what you may afford with getting blades that will not let you down when it really counts.

Marketing is almost as deceitful as politics, so do not believe everything you read in an advertisement. Manufacturers frequently change names of steels to make buyers think it is a new type of steel (example: 440B, AUS-8, and A8 are the same steel). Distributers will advertise things like "high carbon 420 stainless steel", which is a lie. Some steel has different names in different countries and advertisers exploit this often. And some manufacturers save money by not doing their own heat treating; they outsource that to a centralized company that puts blades from many manufacturers in its furnaces. A master knife maker would never leave it to a stranger to temper his steel.

For those reasons, do a little research before you give your money to a knife distributor. Over my lifetime I have carried a lot of knives and put them to the test on 3 continents. The following is a short list, in no particular order, of popular knife companies that I believe make good to outstanding higher-end production knives (they do make low-end budget knives in their lineup too though) that are of acceptable quality off the shelf and are sold around the world:

- RAT Cutlery
- KA-BAR
- Ontario Knives
- Boker
- Bear & Son Cutlery
- Gerber
- Buck
- Kershaw
- Benchmade
- CRKT

Should you bother with cheap budget knives at all? My counter question would be, 'how cheap'? I say your primary knives should be the best you can afford. Your backup knives should be of the best quality you think is reasonable. After that, your extra knives you can save a few dollars. I look at knives the way I look at firearms; I have my high-quality expensive firearms and I also have specialty backup firearms, but I also keep a few cheap guns like SKS, Mosin, etc available just in case. I could never afford for all my extra firearms to be of the quality of my primaries, and the same is true of my knives. Use the 5th Principle of Patrolling.

Do not forget to make a field sharpening kit. In the woods I always keep a Gerber Diamond Sharpener in my pocket. It is the size of an ink pen, costs $10 USD, and one of mine has lasted over 8 years of frequent use. I keep one in the tackle boxes, in each bug-out bag, in my vehicles, on my ATV, etc. These sharpeners will re-sharpen a blade to acceptable hone very quick. They can sharpen serrations, a broad head, or fishing hook too.

Also in the bug-out bags I keep two small (1"x3"x1/2") Arkansas stones: a course stone and a fine stone. I also keep a thin porcelain rod and a 5"x5" piece of stropping leather for razor-sharp finish work. For my ax, hatchet, tomahawk, etc, I keep a small bastard file and a semi-course synthetic finishing stone. With these I can sharpen my blades at the end of each day to hones better than factory new. (Many times while camping I have offered knife/ax sharpening service to novice campers as a trade for luxury items like toilet paper or a cup of coffee.)

11. Survival Firearms

"Bushido is all very well in its way, but it is no match for a 30-06." COL Jeff Cooper

I have never bought into the concept that a firearm is just a tool. That line of logic claims that a gun is like any other machine that enhances the ability to work, like a hammer, drill, saw or etc, thus is just as innocent as those machines. It is true that a firearm does mechanically increase a person's ability to accomplish a task, but the task of the firearm is not to build but to destroy. A firearm is designed to be a weapon that kills meat and enemies. Beyond that simple fact, I see absolutely no reason to justify why a free man requires a weapon. I see no reason to hide behind rhetoric or sugarcoat the thing. Weapons are a fact of life and the need to kill food and to provide security is the reason why.

People do not pay for elaborate engravings on tools. Dictators do not fear people armed with tools. Tools do not kill game. Tools do not protect women and children in the night. Tools do not liberate the enslaved. Only weapons do these things and we need to know the difference. If you must justify why you need a weapon verses a tool, you are talking to the wrong folks anyways.

Any firearm can be used to some extent for survival purposes; however, some are more preferred than others. Guns built entirely for self-defense tend to be good at that but not as good for hunting. Guns built solely for hunting are good for hunting but may be much less desirable for self-defense. The trick is to select the type of firearms that can fill both roles as required. And always keep in mind that one gun can never really do it all; different circumstances will demand different weapons.

Ammunition is a major factor. Availability is more important than power, size, etc. The calibers in your arsenal need to be highly common, thus more easily replenished. If all your guns are rare, exotic, obsolete, or "wildcat" calibers, you are going to have trouble. Can you stock up thousands of rounds? Yes, but if your ammo stash gets compromised or your reloading supplies get stolen you will only have what you can find by other means.

Safety: These rules are written in blood.

1. Always treat every firearm like it is loaded.

2. NEVER point the gun at something you do not want to kill or destroy.

3. Keep your finger off the trigger until you are going to fire.

4. Always keep the firearm on safe until you are going to fire.

5. Never carry the firearm with the safety off.

6. Know your target and what is beyond it.

The Mighty .22 Long Rifle: Many woodsmen rightfully consider the venerable .22 LR to be the ultimate survival caliber. It may not be as efficient as center-fire cartridges, but in a pinch it is plenty adequate. For the price of around a dozen aluminum arrows, you can purchase around 1,000 .22 LR rounds; each of which is as lethal as an arrow at twice the range. And a box of 500 .22 LR bullets can be held in one hand. (Try that with .300 Win Mags.)

Yet despite its small size the .22 LR is lethal all out of proportion to its price and size. This cartridge has killed pretty much everything that walks, crawls, flies, and many things that swim. It has been documented to have killed walruses, bears, moose, and even African elephant. In many places it is a preferred caliber for deer poachers because it is plenty effective without the noise of center-fire calibers. It will kill a man hundreds of meters beyond its practical aiming range.

You may have considered before what the ultimate survival weapon would be. Perhaps something you can build on your own like a spear, slingshot, bow, or atlatl. But in the time you are trying to make arrows, you can already be hunting indefinitely with a shoe-box full of .22 LR ammo. When surviving, every minute is a commodity.

It may be the most common caliber on Earth. Another factor is, unlike some other calibers, the more rural you travel (away from urban areas) the more likely you are to find more .22 LR ammo.

The .22 LR is relatively quiet and has no recoil. Children and new shooters can quickly learn to shoot proficiently with such a firearm. More fundamentals can be learned in one day with a .22 LR than in a decade with a 30-06.

Every survivalist should own a few .22 LR weapons. In my household I keep a .22 LR handgun and rifle for every family member and around 1,000 rounds per firearm. In an emergency every member can harvest everything from rabbits to deer and defend from two-legged predators too.

Training Note: When I was a small boy, the first .22 that was put in my hands was a Marlin Model 60. It was almost as tall as me and that was what I had to learn to shoot with.

When I began teaching my own kids to shoot I made certain to give them .22's that fit their size. By far, the best youth .22's I found for my money were Crickett .22 rifles. These little lightweight, single-shot rifles are perfect. They come in .22LR and .22 Win Mag. The customer service at Crickett is also outstanding.

Rifles: A man with a rifle can forge his own fate. The rifle really is spades. If the enemy has a rifle, you do not want to be the guy only holding a pistol.

My primary considerations with rifles are durability and commonality of caliber. After that is accuracy, but I find that quality rifles are always inherently more accurate than the human firing them.

My five main rifle calibers are: 5.56mm, 7.62x39mm, 30-30 Win, .308 Win, and 30-06. These are not the only calibers I keep, but are my primary focus because they are extremely common (easy to replenish) and very well suited for what they do. Are there other options? Yes of course; I am only saying these five will serve you well.

5.56mm- I carried this caliber in combat and know firsthand that it works. Anyone that says it is a puny caliber is full of bullshit. The beauty of this cartridge is that you get an effective rifle, with low recoil, and for every 7 rounds of .30 cal/7.62mm you can carry 11 rounds of 5.56mm.

The AR platform lends very well to both hunting and self-defense. The ammo and magazines are extremely plentiful. Bulk ammo is currently to be had for a bargain. (Even during the US ammo famines of 2009 and

2012, I was still scooping up 5.56mm deals.) I mainly stock Federal 55 grain or 62 grain.

7.62x39mm- The Russians dumped this cartridge back in 1980 for the 5.45x39mm, but by then 7.62x39mm was so popular all over the world that it was never going away. With a jacketed soft-point (JSP) bullet it has almost the exact ballistics of a 30-30 Win, but from a high-capacity, semi-automatic platform. Recoil is low and ammo is very cheap. I like it because with full metal jacket (FMJ) ammo you have a deep penetrating military round, but with JSP ammo you have a good hunting round.

30-30 Win- This humble cartridge is often overlooked by modern gun enthusiasts, but it nearly left species like the white-tailed deer and grizzly bear extinct. Before super-magnums hit the scene, this simple cartridge had already harvested more game than all the other new super-magnums would harvest combined. It is very common in North America and almost any small-town hardware store stocks it.

The 30-30 makes a pretty good defensive rifle too. It is most commonly chambered in the very solid and proven Marlin 336 or Winchester 94 rifles. These rifles handle easy, fire quick, and you do not need to worry about magazines. You can quickly reload as you go.

.308 Win- Probably the most practical center-fire rifle cartridge you can have. Recoil is moderate, hits hard enough at long range and most of the best bolt-action and semi-auto rifles have variants chambered for this cartridge. Some consider this the finest military round ever made, which accounts for why it is used worldwide; it holds its own as a great big-game cartridge too.

30-06 (Springfield)- Some would correctly argue this old cartridge is the most versatile center-fire ever made. Anything a .308 Win can do, the 30-06 can do just a bit better, but without magnum recoil or blast. It can be loaded all the way down for varmints or all the way up to grizzly bear. The list of loads for this round is pages long. And it is common around the world; I have encountered this cartridge in commercial/sporting use on three continents. Another cartridge almost always stocked in small-town hardware stores.

And five rifle calibers that deserve honorable mention for superb track records and/or availability:

- .270 Win
- 7mm Rem Mag
- .243 Win
- .300 Win Mag
- .45-70

Carbines: A carbine is often a shorter version of a full-sized rifle (i.e. an M4 versus an M16). Or it can be built from the start as a short, lightweight, handy rifle (i.e. an M1 Carbine). The caliber does not specifically define a carbine—it may be chambered for rifle or pistol round. Typically a *rifle* has a 20" (500mm) barrel while a *carbine* has 16" (400mm) or less. Any length in between is open to argument. In general though, a true carbine will always have the relative characteristics mentioned before: short, lightweight, and handy. You carry a carbine when you need portability more than range, but more firepower than a handgun.

For rifle caliber carbines I generally stick to 5.56mm, 7.62x39mm, and 30-30 Win. These cartridges remain very manageable in a carbine platform and still perform at an acceptable ballistic level. A .308 Win and 30-06 are more manageable to shoot and do best from a 20"-24" barreled rifle.

The beauty of a carbine is that it can be chambered for handgun cartridges and give you commonality of ammunition between your handgun and longarm. For magnum revolver cartridges (.357 Mag, .44 Mag, etc.) a carbine length barrel greatly enhances ballistic performance; a 16" barrel roughly adds 500 fps of velocity over a 6" barrel. That means that some hot revolver loads can actually edge in to the lower spectrum of center-fire rifle performance at a range of 100-200 yards. There are .357 Magnum loads that will leave a carbine barrel with as much energy as a factory loaded 30-30 Win load! (Caution: Some hot loads that are safe in a modern carbine can wreck some revolvers; verify that your revolver can withstand the pressure. Ruger Redhawk, Blackhawk, Super Blackhawk and "Old" Vaquero models are a good place to start.)

The Marlin 1894 or clones of the Winchester 92 made by companies like Rossi are probably the most popular carbines chambered for revolver cartridges. My two favorite combinations are a pair of .357 Mag Vaqueros and a Rossi 92 chambered for the same; they will also fire .38 Special all day long. Or a pair of .45 Colt Vaqueros and a Rossi 92 chambered for the same. *If you do not reload*, you may do better to avoid .45 Colt and use .44 Magnums, simply because factory .45 Colt is rather anemic. Only a very few companies, like Buffalo Bore, load .45 Colt up to .44 Magnum power level.

In the semi-auto pistol class (9mm, .45 ACP, etc) you will not get a lot more ballistic performance from the longer barrel. A semi-auto pistol bullet reaches 90% of its potential in the first 3"-5" of barrel length. A 16" carbine barrel will give you roughly 100-200 fps more velocity over your 5" pistol barrel. Does that mean semi-auto carbines are not worth your time? No, it does not mean that at all. It is a fact that the longer sight radius means you will be able to hit a hell of a lot further away than with a pistol. And for recoil-sensitive people, they will find this type of carbine very pleasant to shoot. In urban areas, a pistol round from a carbine is a lot more comfortable to fire in an enclosed space than a rifle cartridge (5.56mm indoors can burst eardrums).

My recommendation for folks who prefer pistol caliber carbines is something like the Just Right Carbine (that is also the name of the manufacturer). It looks like an M4, uses Glock or 1911 magazines, and is chambered in 9mm, .40 S&W, and .45 ACP.

Shotgun: A lot of people will tell you that a shotgun is the ultimate final answer to close-range defense and that there is no argument about that. It is in fact an awesome defense weapon and also an indispensable hunting weapon. But it is not the ultimate final answer to anything; it is just one other solution in a long list of options.

One prevalent myth about shotguns is that you can just "point and shoot". If this myth were true at all, every one of us could learn to be Olympic skeet shooters in one day. Any notion that you do not need to aim a shotgun is completely ridiculous. You do not have to aim it as precisely as a rifle, but you still must aim it.

For the first 3 yards (2.7m) a shotgun load does not expand. After that first 3 yards, it spreads roughly 1" (25mm) per yard it travels. That means at extreme close-range, like in most homes, the pattern will never spread larger than a soup can's lid. That is a far cry from the Hollywood depiction of shotguns peppering entire walls from 20 feet. Even out at 25 yards (23m), most shotgun loads will be roughly less than the width of a grown man from shoulder to shoulder. <u>It is essential to know that you must aim a shotgun</u>; the "point 'n shoot" technique does not work in a fight.

Can you make a shotgun that spreads faster? Yes you can. Simply use a full choke and use shot that is un-plated (soft lead shot). The combination of un-plated lead and a full choke deforms the pellets as they pass through the choke, causing the pellets to lose their sphere shape and therefore fly slightly erratically. The end result is a looser pattern; perhaps 1.5"-2" per yard of flight.

You should be cautioned, however, that a loose shotgun pattern is very counterproductive. A single 00 buckshot pellet has less terminal effect than a .32 ACP bullet. Spreading out the shot too far causes you to lose the effect that makes a shotgun such an effective weapon; that is the effect of nine 00 buckshot pellets simultaneously hitting a relatively small area on the attacker's torso. That is why the military, law enforcement, and the firearms industry still strives to build shotguns and premium ammunition that holds a tight pattern all the way out to 40+ yards (36m).

Another prevailing myth about shotguns is that they are useless except for close range. That is simply not true. A shotgun equipped with ghost-ring sights, even with a smoothbore barrel, can consistently put slugs in a man-sized target even out at 125 yards. (In my old unit we carried 5 slugs on a stock carrier and filled the magazine -1 with buckshot plus buckshot chambered. That empty round in the magazine we called "the ghost round". If you needed a slug, you simply insert it into the ghost round, pumped the buckshot round out of the chamber, and now you had a slug chambered. Throw another slug in the magazine and now you can remove a door from the hinges or engage a threat beyond 100 yard, etc.)

Having said all that, if you do your utmost to fully appreciate the weaknesses and strengths of the shotgun, and train with it to high proficiency, it is a formidable weapon.

I recommend avoiding uncommon shotgun calibers like 10 Gauge (GA), 16GA, and 28GA. There is nothing inherently wrong with them, except their use is totally dwarfed by 12GA, 20GA, and .410 shotguns. Currently 250 rounds of 12GA small game loads sells for only $65 and 15 rounds of 00 buckshot is only

$12.50. Once again, focus on what works and is easy to replenish.

A note about the .410 shotgun is that it is a bit more of a specialty caliber. Despite its small size and light load it still costs as much as its big brothers. It is a good choice for very young shooters or for combination guns like the M6 Scout. I mainly keep .410 around to let the kids learn "shotgunning" with.

A .410 is not a good choice for self-defense revolvers like the Taurus Judge. Three or four low velocity buckshot pellets will never consistently create a wound as big as a .45 Colt hollowpoint. And a .410 slug—that is a .40 caliber slug that weights about 90 grains. Keep in mind a .40 S&W is normally a 165 grain or 180 grain slug. Firing .410 from a revolver is just asking for under-penetration and failure to hit vital organs necessary to stop a threat.

Handguns: Nobody needs a definition of what a handgun is, but there is one reality we should all be clear on: In a disaster scenario, or especially a long-term survival situation, a handgun should never be your primary weapon.

All handguns of practical size are relatively puny weapons; you have to carry something like a .500 S&W Magnum revolver with max pressure loads to have a handgun in the power class of a .308 Win. And truth be told, most .500 S&W owners shoot loads that are less potent than a 30-30 Win. That entirely aside, a handgun just does not have the reach of a rifle or in some cases even a shotgun.

The only reasons handguns exist is simply for portability. There are just times when you cannot work with a longarm in your hands or slung on your back. The handgun offers you reasonable protection strapped to your hip until you can get to your rifle, or in case your rifle catastrophically fails! I think of a handgun like my reserve parachute; I am glad to have it but would rather use the main chute.

A fighting handgun (.45 ACP, 9mm, .38 Special, etc) does not stop or kill a threat the way a rifle does. A rifle rapidly stops or kills by crushing a devastating would channel while at the same time delivering enough kinetic energy to burst blood vessels, rupture organs, shatter bone, and rip apart tissue. You need to have over 1,000 foot-pounds of energy where the bullet hits the meat to even begin to be in the threshold of rifle class power. A practical fighting handgun is lucky to even produce half that energy at the muzzle. Therefore, a handgun works more like an arrow than a rifle in the mechanics of stopping a threat. The handgun bullet relies on its ability to use its momentum to puncture deep into the threat, thereby crushing blood vessels which will cause a rapid drop in blood pressure that makes the threat stop, lose consciousness, and possibly die.

I classify my handguns in 3 categories:

- Backup
- Defense
- Multipurpose

Backup- Some folks call these a BUG (Back Up Gun). They are the sub-compact class of handgun. Usually the size of a snubnose revolver, Glock 26, Walther PPK, Kel-Tec P3, Berretta Tomcat, etc, depending on the occasion.

A backup handgun is exactly what it sounds like: A small handgun used as a last ditch weapon when your other weapons fail or get knocked from your control.

Backup handguns are also sometimes the only handgun you can carry fully concealed when you absolutely must appear unarmed. And sometimes they are insurance in case you are searched; they may stop searching when they find the first handgun. This last point is a major consideration in a survival situation; you have to plan for any possibility.

Common calibers are .38 Special, 9mm Luger, .380 ACP, .32 ACP, and .25 ACP.

I avoid .22LR in this category unless it is a revolver. There are two reasons. First, a .22LR is rimfire primed, which is not as a reliable ignition source as center-fire primers. It is a fact that one out of every few hundred .22LR fail to fire. A revolver you can just pull the trigger again, but in a pistol you now have a stoppage. Second, from a 2" barrel, a .25 ACP and a .22LR have effectively the exact same ballistics.

For .32 ACP and .25 ACP you are better off avoiding hollowpoints and instead using FMJ or solids. The tiny holes in hollowpoints of these calibers typically clog with clothing and fail to expand. Even if they do expand, the lightweight bullets once expanded do not have the momentum to puncture deep enough to hit vital organs or major blood vessels. By using FMJ bullets you at least have consistent deep penetration.

Defense- These are your mid-size to full-size handguns like the Glock 19/23, 1911A1, Beretta 92, Springfield XD, S&W

Model 10, etc. This is a weapon light enough for constant carry, small enough to conceal if necessary, reasonable capacity for its design, and a sensible amount of power that can be controlled. Its primary mission is a defensive weapon that is always worn on your body. For example: My daily concealed carry weapon is my Glock 19. In a disaster situation that fact would not change, except that I probably would no longer conceal it.

You probably would not hunt with your defensive handgun, but in an emergency you could harvest a dog, cat, or deer at close range. But the principal purpose of this weapon is always foremost to quickly stop other dangerous people.

These are the calibers I recommend:

- 9mm Luger (9x19, 9mm Para)
- .45 ACP (11.43mmx23mm)
- .40 S&W (10mm, but not 10x25mm or 10mm Auto)
- .38 Special (9x29R)
- .357 Magnum (9x33R)
- .44 Special
- .45 Colt

The calibers listed are plenty sufficient for defense and are common enough in North America to be easily replenished. Some calibers may be scarcer in other places though. Depending where you live in the world .38 Super may be more common than .45 ACP because military rounds may be banned. In Australia and Canada .40 S&W is a Law Enforcement round, thus somewhat common, but in Europe it has only caught on in a couple areas in very limited amounts, while in the US it is an extremely common cartridge. In the UK .45 Colt ammunition is nonexistent, but in Italy the cowboy enthusiasts shoot it fairly often. You can also fire .45 Schofield in your .45 Colt (during the last ammo shortage I was finding Schofield fairly regularly in Texas).

The most common center-fire pistol cartridge on Earth is easily the 9mm Luger. There is probably not a modern nation on the planet where either the police or military do not use 9mm. In the past decade, even China and former Soviet countries have converted over to the 9mm Luger cartridge for some pistols and sub-machineguns. In many parts of South America, military rifle cartridges (5.56mm, etc) are illegal, so the security contractors use 9mm carbines. From Iran to South Africa to Turkey to Japan, and the list goes on, if you find pistol ammunition it will most likely be 9mm Luger.

In the US, the 9mm, .45 ACP, .40 S&W, and .38 Special are the most common handgun ammunition; not necessarily in that order depending where you live. There is probably enough of these cartridges laying around in closets and dressers to last a century, which is a good thing because these calibers are all very good for their purpose. Also consider the weight of ammunition; it adds up fast. You can carry a lot more 9mm that .45 ACP.

Multipurpose- Sometimes you need handguns that can pull double duty. Good examples are the Ruger Mark III pistols I keep in all my bug-out bags. These pistols are there in case I am separated from my other firearms, they are useful to hunt small game, and since I have several I could trade the extra ones for medicine or etc later if necessary.

Another example is my .357 Mag and .45 Colt revolvers (you may prefer .44 Mag, .41 Mag, etc). These are fine defensive revolvers, but since I mainly stick to rural areas, if my rifle breaks, these revolvers are sufficient intermediate weapons until I get to another rifle. From a steady rest these revolvers will hit a man-size target at 100 yards or bring down a large deer. I cannot always carry a second rifle, but I can carry a handgun with sufficient characteristics to improve my odds if my rifle is damaged.

On my ATV rack, I keep a Glock 17 with four extra 32-round magazines. I think of this as my "get the hell out of Dodge" pistol. I consider this a multipurpose pistol because in addition to performing other pistol duties, it is capable of throwing down a high volume of fire with one hand.

Firearm Carry Accessories: This is one of my pet peeves: A guy buys more guns than the local National Guard armory and buys nothing to hump any of it around with.

A good rifle sling can save your life. That is why I put a sling on all my longarms, including shotguns.

If you get hit by a bullet, your hands reflexively open and then clinch, this will leave your rifle in the dirt. Now you have to pick it up or leave it while you are being shot at. If you fall while running, your hands instinctively open wide, which will send your rifle flying out of reach. Ever try to drag a wounded person and maintain control of both your rifles? All that can be avoided by a good 1-point or 2-point sling.

   *Avoid 3-point slings. These usually put a useless nylon strap down the length of your weapon. With an AR, that strap gets in the way of your bolt release. On some rifles/carbines/SMG the strap interferes with your charging handle. Either way you get an extra strap that can catch on anything you walk by. And 3-point slings are slow and complicated to adjust.

   The best slings I ever used in the military were the VTAC sling (now made by 5.11) and the slings made by Vickers Tactical. These slings are tough and have the fastest adjust I know of. If you can find the older slings with metal furniture, get those. Plastic fittings work fine, but eventually the sunlight will weaken them until they are brittle. I put 100mph tape over the plastic fittings so they last longer. In extreme cold they may still crack though.

   Proper wear of a 1-point or 2-point sling places the butt of the weapon as close to your armpit as it can get. When you let the weapon go, it should hang in the "low ready position". I prefer a VTAC 2-point because I can quickly loosen it to throw the rifle behind me in order to use both my hands to perform a task.

Carrying a bunch of magazines in your pockets sucks. Do not overlook buying several magazine pouches and then buy a few extra. It is a good idea to have different styles so you can reconfigure to different options as you see necessary. Pouches also wear out. I have walked around enough wearing pouches that I had M4 magazines rub holes through the bottom of the pouches. Nylon tends to last longer than cotton canvas. Leather will last a long time but requires maintenance. Always either buy military surplus or quality kit from places like Blackhawk.

Use the same logic with handgun holsters and knife sheaths. Do not limit yourself to one style of carry. As time goes by you will find that you prefer different modes of carry in different situations.

Sights: If you are not familiar with "peep sights" or "peep aperture sights", I highly recommend you take a look at them. With all my rifles, carbines, and shotguns that I realistically can convert, I change their conventional iron sights to peep aperture sights.

The world seems to favor the sphere or circle. The solar system is round. The planet is round. The sun is round. And your pupil is round. A peep aperture sight just fits right in. The reason peep aperture sights work so well is that your pupil naturally lines up everything in the circle of the peep sight perfectly. The only way to screw it up is to try to over-think it. As far as iron sights are concerned, peep aperture sights are as fast and efficient as it can get.

For my lever-actions and Ruger 10/22's, I use Skinner Sights. They are a tough, metal machined sight that is affordable and very easy to install. The manufacturer, Skinner Sights LLC, provides an abundance of information and directions to help you get exactly what you need. They have a long list of weapons that they build specific peep aperture sights for. I found this company by accident about 4 years ago and they get two thumbs up from this old Soldier.

For my shotguns I use Trijicon ghost rings. For AK variants without a rail and SKS I use Mojo Sights. Mojo sights replace the existing U-notch sight. Some folks do not like Mojo because the peep aperture is still pretty far from the eyeball. An alternative is made by Tech Sights, that puts the peep in a more traditional rifle location, but you must replace the dust cover and you lose the quick takedown of the factory dust cover. If it has a rail I prefer the Texas Weapon System rear aperture, and you can put the sight wherever you prefer.

Cleaning/Lubricant: A portable cleaning kit is essential. The old M16 cleaning kits in a rectangle pouch are pretty good; the more modern Otis kits are vastly better. Or you can make your own kit by rolling a toothbrush, snake, and small bottle of oil in an old shirt. You can even make a snake by tying some knots in 550 and pulling that through the bore.

For weapon lube, avoid the "dry lube" such as graphite powders. There is really no such thing as a dry lubricant and they offer no protection from rust like oils will. Military CLP is decent oil and can be found in large bulk. You can also find Arctic Weight CLP, which is heavier and works better in every season. Hoppe's and RemOil are good oil and have pretty advanced products. Outstanding oil is made by MilTech; it is highly advanced and made to keep rifles going in bad conditions. If you want to go cheap, there is nothing wrong with 3-IN-ONE® oil; it works great and comes in handy square bottles.

12. Optics

Do you have to have optics to survive? No, but they sure can make life easier. It is easier to study something from 500 yards away than to risk walking to within 50 yards to make a decision about it. The earlier you detect something the more reaction time you have. Remember that dead people rarely ever saw what killed them. And seeing something is about multiple perspectives. Magnified optics, whether they are binoculars, monocular, or a rifle scope put another perspective at your fingertips.

One caveat is that placing optics on firearms does not make everyone a better shooter. A poor marksman with iron sights will also be a poor marksman with an optical sight. Some basic fundamentals of marksmanship like steady position, trigger squeeze, breathing, and follow through are not magically corrected by an optical sight. The only basic fundamental that really changes is sight alignment when you transition from iron sights to optical sights. Many people try to answer training questions with technological answers and are frustrated by bad results; this is the perfect example of such. No expensive state-of-the-art scope can replace mastering marksmanship fundamentals.

For simplicity I divide optics in to four categories:

- Day Observation
- Night Observation
- Day Sights
- Night Sights

*Note: Night optics is covered in Chapter 13.

Day Observation- Lifting a rifle to use your scope gets old pretty fast. A pair of compact 10X power binoculars really goes a long way. They only weight a few ounces and you can glass an area for long periods without fatigue. You can also study someone else from a distance without assuming a highly hostile posture.

Just as useful is a monocular. They are half the size and weight of comparable binoculars. The tradeoff is you may lose some depth perception, however, many people prefer a monocular.

There was a time when you had to buy expensive German or Switzerland built binoculars to get outstanding quality. It is still true that you get what you pay for, but advances in manufacturing have closed the gap a lot. If you want to buy a $1,000 pair of binoculars, go ahead and you will undoubtedly be pleased with them. I have used such and they really are awesome. But I have also carried my own personal $100 compact binoculars for years, hunting and in combat zones, and never had any problem with them. I also keep a few $50 "Wal-Mart" binoculars around and they work fine too.

Full-size binoculars give you a better view with more detail, but the tradeoff is weight. Believe me; you will get tired of humping them around. I recommend full-size binoculars for static or permanent positions, like your guard point or an overwatch area. If the distance is great enough, a powerful spotting scope (like from the range) may even be better.

Day Sights- There is a lot of advantages to using optics on your longarms. Everything from long-range fire to extreme close-range fire can be enhanced, just depending on what weapon/optic combination you are going for. Because there are so many variables, we will only focus on rifles/carbines with the intent of long-range, close-range, and general-purpose fire.

*Note that I did not mention *"extreme long-range"* fire. If your intent is to put a 6mm bullet in an SR1 target one mile away (1,600m), then you have a lot more books to start reading.

Long-Range- Terrain always dictates, but for most of us this is 300m-800m. Scopes dedicated to this task should be variable power, in the neighborhood of 3X-9X power. Anything greater than 10X power is overkill for this. Tube diameter should be at least 1" but 30mm is better. A 40mm objective lens is optimal. If you go much smaller, you lose some detail and light gathering. If you go much larger you will be forced to mount the scope higher over the bore.

Eye relief should be between 3"-5" for these rifles, but what is comfortable is shooter preference; the greater the recoil, the more eye relief you will want. A 3" eye relief scope on a .300 Win Mag can cut your eyebrow, but you would never know it mounted on a 5.56mm.

Reticle preference is subjective, but the most practical is a duplex reticle. Some folks think they need a "mil-dot" reticle (milliradian), but if you are not going to get training on how to use it, then it is not going to be very helpful.

I have been using Leupold scopes for hunting rifles since I was in high school and in the US Army too, so that is naturally what I recommend. For my long-range AR, I mount a MOD 1 3-9x40mm. For my long-range bolt-action I mount an M3 3.5-10x40mm. You can purchase these scopes specific to certain calibers, like 5.56mm, .308 Win, .300 Win Mag etc.

Will a deer rifle scope work for long-range fire? Absolutely! Just make sure it is as close as possible to the characteristics I mentioned earlier and if you do your part, you can hit at reasonably long-range. Most of my bolt-action deer rifles have a 2-7x40mm Leupold of one model or another mounted on them. I rarely hunt over 200 yards, but in a pinch they can hit a lot further.

Close-Range- These sights are often called "reflexive sights" because they are primarily intended for rapid instinctive (aka reflexive) fire. If a threat suddenly emerges at 10 meters away, these are the sights you want.

The reason these sights work is because they are "parallax free". No matter how you look through a zeroed parallax free sight, the point of aim will still be on the point of impact at a factory designated range (usually 50m). You can hold the weapon upside down or place the butt in the center of your chest; it does not matter, as long as you see the dot that is where the bullet will hit at 50m. It makes accurate fire from your weak hand very easy. If a sight is not parallax free this cannot work; every time you look through a normal sight differently, the angle difference will change the point of aim vs. point of impact.

What is parallax? An easy demonstration goes like this: Close your left eyes and hold your pointer finger out and conceal an object across the room (light switch, cup, etc). Without moving your finger, close your right eye, now open the left eye. Now you can see the object. This is how parallax affects most conventional sights. The effect is so strong that zeroing a rifle with iron sights while the sun is to your left can cause your point of impact to slightly change when the sun is to the right, or vice versa.

Reflexive sights also have unlimited eye relief, because they are not magnified. You can mount one on a pistol, shotgun, or rifle just the same. It does not matter if your eye is 3 inches or 3 feet from the optic, it looks the same.

The drawback of reflexive sights is they require batteries. This is normally not an issue, but in a long-term survival situation, you will need a way to replenish or recharge batteries.

It is a consideration that reflexive sights are not magnified. They are designed to give you a wide field of view up close and to be fired with both eyes open for maximum situational awareness. Does this mean you cannot engage beyond close range with these sights? No, it does not at all. I routinely fired reflexive sights out to 300m in training. I witnessed Soldiers shooting silhouettes at ranges I dare not say here for fear you would not believe me.

EOTECH makes popular holographic reflexive sights. These are boxy-shaped and mount well on weapons with top rails. I have used the 512 and 552 models and find the lenses on the EOTECH to be somewhat exposed, but most folks do not see this as an issue. They are made with a variety of reticles, from 1MOA dots to larger dots and dots with circles, and in green or red. In my opinion the

1MOA red dot is superior. The red dot on the
552 is compatible with night vision.

The strength of the EOTECH is that it
runs on AA batteries, which are extremely
common. They will work with rechargeable
batteries. I advise always using lithium
batteries for sights. Lithium batteries last much
longer, are less affected by temperature, and
have a more consistent power output over the
charge lifespan. (Alkaline batteries taper off,
but lithium puts out the same right up until the
charge dies.)

AIMPOINT makes my favorite
reflexive sights. The Army calls them the M68
CCO. Commercially they are called Comp M2,
M3, or M4. I started out on the Comp M2,
which I loved, and by the time they were
fielding the Comp M4 they almost perfected
my favorite sight.

These reflexive sights are round and
look more like a short traditional scope. I find
them to be very tough and they can take a lot of
abuse. The Comp M2 and M3 run on tiny
lithium batteries called DL1/3N or 2L76. These
batteries last a long time but can be very hard
to find.

The Comp M4 corrected the odd battery issue and runs on one AA battery.

M68's are compatible with night vision. We figured out pretty fast that we could improve night sights by mounting the M68 forward of a PVS-14. It works. An M68 also has a 3X adapter that can be attached for magnification.

AIMPOINT optics is also very effective with a back-up sight (BUS). I recommend MAGPUL MBUS sights if your weapon is not already equipped.

Training Note: On most combat longarms (AR, AK, FN etc) you can mechanical zero the reflexive sight to the iron sights before you start zeroing with live ammo. Simply look through the reflexive sight and move the dot with the adjustment turrets until the dot sits on the front sight post like a marble in the middle of a table. Now your first shots should be on paper.

Here is a simple zero for 5.56mm reflexive sights: You use a target at 25m to zero. If your point of impact is 1.5" low at 25m, it will be 1.5" high at 100m, then dead on at 200m, and about a foot low at 300m, depending on barrel length and bullet weight. This means from 0m-300m you can hit with a center mass hold.

For every 10m closer than 50m, your point of impact will be roughly 1" low. That means at 10m away, you aim at their hair to hit their face/ocular cavity.

It is always a good idea to confirm zero at 50m, 100m, and 200m. Be advised though that your group will open up, so out at 100m+ you triangulate the groups.

Most people accustomed to magnified rifle scopes require adjustment to properly firing with reflexive sights. You aid this transition by training with the objective lens covered with a cap or tapped on paper. This forces the shooter to keep both eyes open.

Your brain will superimpose the red dot in the sight that your right eye sees onto the target picture your left eye sees. Practice rapidly engaging multiple targets from 10m to 50m like this. After a few training sessions the shooter will instinctively use the sight with both eyes open. CAUTION: Close-range fire has ricochet hazards. Only use targets and ammunition intended for close-range training.

General-Purpose- These types of sights excel at ranges from 50m to 600m.

Once again, if you have to you can use a deer rifle scope for this. Nothing says you must buy a $1,000 military scope. Everyone has different circumstances and requirements.

For many years my favorite general-purpose AR scope was the Colt 4x20mm. The first one I got as part of a trade. I liked it so much I found a couple more for around $200 each. These scopes are simple, tough, and work great on anything from an AK to FN LAR to whatever. If you want a good scope that easily transitions from urban to rural terrain during daytime, there is nothing wrong with this style of scope. It is not meant to hit a gnat in the teeth at 800m, and it will not, but it will hit a man-sized or deer-sized target at 400m all day long.

Right now the summit of general-purpose military scopes is the Trijicon ACOG. Initially I was very pessimistic about ACOG's, but after years of working with them I now admit they are as tough as they get and have a lot of genius in their design.

You buy them matched to caliber and barrel length; you can find most NATO calibers from 5.56mm to .50 BMG. It is not a night sight, but you can see part of the reticle in the dark without batteries because of the fiber-optic setup it uses (they do have a battery operated version). They have different reticles, but the most popular in the Army is the red chevron. Magnification is fixed and can be had from 3X to 6X, but 4X is the most popular.

A "chevron" is an upside-down "V". In the ACOG reticle the chevron has a post under it with 5 graduated marks for range. If the top tip of the chevron is zeroed for 100m, halfway down the chevron, or the top of the inside, is 200m. The top of the post under that is 300m, and each graduated mark is another 100 for a total of 800m.

The outside of the ACOG has a long fiber-optic tube on it. During daylight this absorbs so much light that the chevron burns a bright orange shape in your vision that lasts an hour. To remedy this, cover the tube with 100mph tape during daytime, and then peel the tape back as it gets dark.

13. Darkness

"Fights are not won by the best—fights are lost by the worst." –Training Proverb

As an infantryman, almost everything we trained to do during the day, we waited until night and did it again in the dark. Around 40% of our training was at night. It was tedious but I learned early on why we spent the time doing it. Everything is much more difficult in the dark. Something that takes 60 seconds in daylight can take 5 minutes to do in the dark. Also, the only way to know if your equipment and techniques works in certain conditions is to use it extensively in those conditions.

Fighting is hard work. Fighting in the dark is even harder. And whoever is more proficient at night fighting has a colossal advantage over anyone not proficient at it. And it is not just about fighting. Everything from navigation to first aid is harder in the dark. Routine tasks become challenging efforts.

It shocked me when I began to associate with civilian survival and combat training. (Civilian includes law enforcement too, because police are also civilians. They can turn in their badge and go home anytime they choose.) I do not exaggerate; it really shocked me. Around 99% of the civilian training I have encountered is during daylight or in high visibility situations.

Civilians treat night training like an alien concept. Please understand I am not putting down anybody. I am not trying to insult anyone or say anyone is better than anybody else. I am only saying what I honestly have seen and thought.

What good is 99% of your training in daylight if 50% of the time in a survival/disaster situation will be at night? That is like learning to swim in a pool without water. Roughly half of our lives it is night. That will not change just because a catastrophe changes society as we now know it.

It would be nice to believe that in the onset of a catastrophe we can go to bed that night and then deal with the new world the next day, but that is not likely. If we have that luxury then it is not that much of an emergency. No, when the sun sets we will still be in harm's way.

As society already is, statistics say violent crime between strangers increases when the sun goes down. (But if you get murdered, overwhelming odds say it will be by someone very personally close to you...food for thought.) Some predators always have come out at sunset and that will never change.

One thing I learned in Third World countries was that the position of the sun in the sky has little influence on whether or not you must work in the dark. When the power goes out manmade structures become darker than night inside. Even at high noon, a stairwell, hallway, garage, basement, utility room, etc of almost any structure (especially large structures) gets very dark.

Planning- Not planning to survive is planning to die. Planning is our most powerful tool. We should already have a rough plan about what to do if "Name the Cataclysm Here" happens when we are: Home, Work, Commuting, Shopping, School, Visiting, etc, etc, etc. Remember PACE planning? (Chapter 2) In every step of PACE planning we should look at how darkness will affect the plan and then anticipate the best solutions.

Considerations include:

- How dark is my building at work/school with no power?
- Must I travel under bridges or tunnels to go home?
- What if my escape plan takes until dark to complete?
- How dark is my home without power?
- How dark is my survival retreat without power?
- Can I navigate my work/home/retreat property in total darkness?
- Can my family members find their way in the dark?
- How can we silently (covertly) communicate in the dark?
- How "blacked out" is my retreat? Can you see the interior lights from outside?
- What do my fields of fire look like at night? Can I see threats?
- What night capabilities do my threats possess?
- What to do if a total power failure happens while I am in a hospital, subway, etc?

This is also where we look at how challenges unique to darkness can be solved by *tactics*, *techniques*, and *procedures* (Chapter 1). Where does dealing with darkness fit in my overall *strategy*? Since half my time on Earth it is night, I will have to deal with it.

Low Light Basics- Your eyes are amazing sensory organs. A healthy adult can go from daylight to full night vision in about 20 minutes. (A person with low vitamin A or using nicotine can take over 30 minutes.) As this happens though, some things in the eyes change.

Whichever way you look at our origins, our first ancestors lived in a garden full of fruit. The ability to see Red and differentiate it from Green leaves was vital to staying will fed. Because we are made to see Red, our visible color spectrum is much greater than the Greenish-Gray vision of most other mammals. We can see the tiniest deviations in colors.

But as light fades the part of our eyes that see colors change to gather more light. As this happens our vision becomes varying shades of Gray. The very center of our vision goes virtually Black.

During daylight we look directly at an object to discern it. We must understand that in the dark that will not work. In the dark or very low light our peripheral vision is vastly more sensitive than our center vision. Because of this, our scanning techniques must change in the dark.

- Constantly, slowly moving our head is more important in the dark, to allow our peripheral vision to gather more data.
- Instead of looking directly at an object, move your eyes in a circular or figure-8 pattern around the object.

In the dark, many other physical and physiological things happen. People in the dark often look straight ahead. When they hear a noise, they often look around and slightly upwards. You can test this by blindfolding a friend and observe them as they navigate around the house. As light decreases, you mind compensates by heightening the sensitivity of your ears. Night air also becomes denser as it cools and transfers sound further. These factors mean that we must change our movement techniques in the dark.

- Move slowly and pause often to listen.
- Avoid moving near walls. Not only does this avoid making scraping noise, but bullets ricochet off walls at half the angle they strike at. The further from the wall, the less likely to get hit.
- When you pause to listen, get low to the ground. You can silhouette anyone nearby against starlight or any light entering the windows.
- If you think they are looking, be still. Human eyes are sensitive to movement in the dark.
- In all but absolute darkness there are still shadows. Always pause to listen in the shadows. This is especially important when there is moonlight.

**If for some reason you do turn on a light at night, keep it pointed down and turn it off as soon as you no longer need it.

Sometimes we must transition from daylight to darkness in short time. If you anticipate going from daylight in to a dark structure, or going from light to dark, there are ways to shorten the transition to night vision or have better vision overall.

- Wear gray or red sunglasses while outside in daylight.
- Take your vitamins.
- Do not look at light sources or stare into the fire.
- LED lights work in the Blue spectrum and take your eyes much longer to recover from than incandescent lights.
- Pirates wore an eye patch so that when they ran below deck they had one eye adjusted to the dark.
- Dim the dashboard as low as you can work with.
- Treat your glasses or eye protection with Rain-X or anti-fog chemical to prevent fogging. Glass gets cool in the dark and your sweat vapor condenses on the glass. (Spit works a little bit too.)

Ammunition- Have you fired your weapons in total darkness? When I test-fire my weapons in the dark, I often find some target and hunting ammunition makes magnificent flashes. You can get a brilliant flame that leaves you seeing a floating orange orb for 5 minutes. Some ammunition throws sparks from the muzzle to the ground! I highly advocate test-firing in the dark. This is especially important if you reload your ammo.

- Shotgun ammunition is usually not a problem unless magnums from short barrels.
- Rifle ammunition start with military surplus, Federal, American Tactical, or Hornady. Almost all military ammo is low flash.
- Military surplus applies to handguns too. Most *premium* self-defense handgun ammo has some degree of flash suppression, but not all. The cheap hollowpoints and the FMJ will often have big flashes. Golden Saber and Hydra-Shok have low flash.

Night Observation/Sights- Having night vision devices (goggles/NVG, device/NVD, optic/NOD, etc) is an immense advantage. You cannot really know the difference unless you use them. Must you have electronic night vision? Only you can answer that. I can tell you this: You do not want the enemy to have it if you do not. I have used night vision so much that at one point I was starting to think the world was green at night.

One of the first things we must understand here is this: DO NOT use night vision recording devices as improvised night sights or night observation devices. Most of those handheld cameras out there with night vision capability are not *passive*. They have an IR flashlight on them. Anybody looking with NVG's will see a bright IR beam glowing. Even if the device has no IR light, it does not have an eye-cup to conceal its display. The light it emits for you to look at the display may as well be a campfire.

For simplicity, let us skip a very long scientific explanation and just say there are two types of night vision devices:

- IR (Infrared)
- Thermal

IR- You must appreciate how sensitive military-style IR night vision is. These gather IR light that you cannot see with your naked eye and available white light (starlight, moonlight, etc) and display it for your eyes many times brighter than it really is. Military-style IR night vision is normally available as goggles, monocular, and weapon sights (scope). Almost all of these you will ever encounter display images in a green-gray picture. They are unique from civilian devices because they are built in a very tough, waterproof shell and they have eyecups that conceal the lens light from getting you detected by other devices.

How sensitive are they? You can see the static sparking on clothes a hundred meters away. If you wash your clothes in detergent with "color brighteners" you appear kind of shiny. If a battle-tank under trees leaves a hatch open, you can see the instrument lights reflecting as a bright glow in the foliage above the turret—this glow is invisible to the naked eye from 10m away, but with IR night vision you can see it perhaps 200m away. In the dark you can see the shadows of clouds passing under starlight. The glowing hand of a wristwatch hand looks like a flaring match. You can see the static on aircraft.

Almost anything that emits a laser beam is highly visible to IR night vision! A range finder, TV remote, certain motion detectors, etc makes a bright arrow leading directly back to you or the device. You may not see it with naked eyes, but IR night vision sees it fine.

If you turn on almost any flashlight, it is visible to military-style IR night vision for a mile away or more. Red or blue filters really do not matter because it still emits IR light that military-style IR night vision is fully capable of seeing.

*The only light commercially available that emits white light visible to your naked eye but invisible to military-style IR night vision is the Phantom lights made by Phantom Products, Inc.

Strength of IR night vision is that if the opposition does not have it, you can covertly do all kinds of things to him. In addition to stealthily sneaking up on someone that cannot see you, or detecting people with poor light disciple, you can covertly signal between mates with IR lights and strobes. You can illuminate an area with IR floodlights and the enemy will not know he is standing in a lit area. You can toss an IR chemlight in a dark room and look inside at people that have no idea the room is bright as day.

The biggest advantage goes both ways though! If you have bad light discipline you are easy preys for people with IR night vision.

IR night vision is available in two styles: *Active* and *Passive*.

Active IR night vision has a built in spotlight or flashlight that emits a beam of IR light that the device uses to see. The device uses the invisible IR beam just like you use a white flashlight. Keep in mind that any enemy NVG sees the light too.

Passive IR night vision does not need to emit an IR beam to see. It gathers available IR and the whole white light spectrum, and then converts it to an image intense enough for you to see almost as well as daytime. Note: Many Passive IR night vision devices are already dual capable; optics like PVS-7B, PVS-14, etc have an IR floodlight that you can switch on as needed. The built in floodlight is only meant for use in absolute darkness, like in a tunnel or basement where there is no starlight. If your device does not have a built in IR light, you can use a separate IR illuminator for total darkness application.

So Goggle vs. Monocular vs. Scope is the next question. Goggles are okay, but I do not like them because they cover both eyes and if the lenses fog up, you are blind; or if you are suddenly exposed to bright white light (which makes NVG's shut off to protect the sensor) you are left blind until you get the goggles of. (A common training ploy is to blind everyone in a room with a flashlight and "kill" them before they remove the dead goggles.) Also, when you pull off goggles you are night-blind for at least 20 minutes.

A scope is great if you want a dedicated night fighter rifle. The drawback is that if you are just observing, you must point a loaded rifle at everybody and everything to look at it.

Monocular is the best compromise in my opinion. If the device dies or the lens fogs, you still have your other eye that can see pretty well. A monocular only makes one eye get night-blind. If you need to look at your watch, radio, etc, you do not need to pull off a monocular like you must with goggles. If you have a sight like an AIMPOINT M68 on your weapon, you can accurately fire the weapon with the monocular and hit an enemy out to about 300m.

What about the cost? It depends if you want Gen 1, Gen 2, Gen 3, or Gen 4, and also what you need it to do. I have used night vision so much that at one point I was starting to think the world was green at night. So to me, I am willing to pay to have some type of capability.

Gen 1: You can buy these for just a couple hundred US dollars. The big problem with Gen 1 is it is 50 year old technology that does not work very well. The field of view is small, as in much smaller than in conventional optics like binoculars. The image has no detail, and they do not work if it is very dark. Even with a bright IR illuminator, you cannot see very far on a dark night.

If you are going to use Gen 1 where there is some light, like in a parking lot where some street lights are nearby or in a building with emergency floodlights on, you can get some use from them. Around a home with light coming from the windows, you can see around the yard. You can discern a chair from a human or a door from a wall. You can detect movement.

In my opinion, during a power blackout, or in the wilderness, Gen 1 is nearly useless.

Gen 2: These are getting into the $1,000 to $2,000 price range. This generation of IR night vision was made infamous during Desert Storm in 1991. The field of view is pretty small, but you can see enough detail to recognize a person up close. Even on a dark night you get some image, even if not a great one. They work fine with an IR illuminator. I feel like these are the minimum useful IR generation and for most folks they are good enough.

Gen 3: Now you are in the $3,000 to $4,000 range. The difference between Gen 3 to Gen 2 is like a plasma TV with Blue-Ray disk to an old tube TV with VHS tapes. It is like comparing an IPod to a cassette walkman. VHS and walkmans worked, but once you get plasma and IPod you do not look back. Gen 3 is like that too.

The field of view is wider. The detail is good enough to read 1" letters from several feet away and read a license plate much further. You can recognize someone you know from over 50m away. Unless it is a cloudy night, you can see very well with detail. This generation is up to the task for almost anything you will want to do.

Gen 4: These go from $5,000 to $10,000. For that you can also get a very nice new 4x4 ATV. I currently use Gen 4 at work, and honestly they have more capability than most folks will really need. It is a bit like buying a Ferrari to drive to work. If you think it is worth it though, you will not be disappointed.

Thermal- A thermal night vision device does not work like IR. Instead of gathering light, it reads thermal radiation.

A few myths about military-style thermal night vision:

- They do not look like in the movie Predator (1987, 20th Century Fox). The image is a very clear black and white image.
- No, you cannot see lights in thermal night vision like in the movie Courage Under Fire (1996, 20th Century Fox). No matter how much you blink a flashlight or headlights at a thermal sight, the viewer will never see it. (In that movie they were confused about what sight an M1 Abrams uses.)
- You cannot see tracers in thermals. The thing is you can see *every* single bullet in the air anyway. The bullets are warmer

than the air, so they are all fully visible with thermal night vision.

- Yes you can actually read signs, license plates, and nametapes with thermals. For some reason you can even see clouds reflecting off of windshield glass.

So how sensitive is thermal night vision? If you stand somewhere awhile your footprints are visible several minutes. If you lay or sit somewhere, the spot is visible after you leave. You can tell if a car has been driven in the last 24 hours. The thermal sights I have at work are so efficient I can tell how much water is in your canteen or camelback. If someone urinates you can see their temperature change and sometimes you can see their breath and sweat vapor.

Thermal sights flip between "white hot" and "black hot" depending on your preference. In "white hot" warm things look brighter and vice versa. Any living thing, even a moth, in your line of sight will glow white in a thermal sight on "white hot".

The big advantage of thermal devices is they pretty much always work, day or night, hot or cold, etc. It can be high noon or you can be in a subway tunnel and thermals still work. You never need to worry about moonlight or total darkness.

The disadvantage is that thermals do not work well in the rain or fog because water absorbs the thermal radiation. There is a brief period during some sunrises and sunsets when radiation washes out your image. Thermals will not see through glass. You can look at a glass/metal/wood/stone structure and tell if it is heated or has air conditioning, but you cannot go to a window and see through the glass. Plants also give off a small amount of heat; if a person gets far enough back in the foliage they may not show up in your sight.

Is there Thermal/IR hybrid? Yes, but as far as I know you need a military contract to buy it.

What is the cost? A civilian thermal handheld camera will get $5,000 dollars or more. A weapon sight will be $8,000 to $25,000 depending how good it is.

Lights- We should start with fighting lights, because they get all the attention anyway. There is a lot of confusion about the right light for the job. About 20 years ago, or less in some cases, the original Mag-Lites (Mag-Lights) and Mini-Mags were being advertised as and used as "tactical tights" or fighting lights. The law enforcement world invented all types of techniques to hold those lights in tandem with a handgun, and even offset the light from the body's vertical axis in an attempt to make the officer less of a target during room clearing. They had to develop techniques to offset the light, quite frankly, because it was not bright enough to blind a threat.

The original Mag-Lites are great. I have plenty of them. They are very tough. But they are not a tactical fighting light. Really they are just a very durable utility light. (Glad to say that Mag-Lite does sell a modern line of updated tactical lights now though.)

A true fighting light is so bright that it is a non-lethal weapon. When you shine it on a dog in a dark yard, the dog will yelp and run away. When you illuminate a threat in a dark room, you do not need to offset this type of light because the threat will be firing with his eyes shut anyway. You should start at around 120 lumens; a light with 200 lumens is optimal. (Lights are used for extreme close-range combat. If you are using a light anywhere else, it will draw fire. Shining any light over distance is a bad idea.)

The next question is incandescent or LED bulb? An LED is very bright but uses less battery power. Incandescent burns the battery faster, but your eyes recover faster from using it than an LED. Because LED mostly uses blue light from the overall spectrum, it makes you night blind longer.

There are a lot of great fighting lights on the market. I can vouch for Surefire because I have been using those since the 1990's. They set the standard for other lights in the same class and I see no reason to change what works.

For handheld, I use a plain Surefire G2 with the 120 lumen lamp installed. The switch is in the perfect spot and it is either on or off. There is no strobe, hi/low, etc to cycle through when you need to burn some retinas and draw a bead. Just pull the light, thumb-press the switch, and you have a brilliant beam of white light. For rail-mounted lights, any of the Surefire X-series is good to go. Rail lights can be had from 150-500 lumens for a decent price.

One of the very best things a civilian can do is to take a "low-light" shooting course. Most cost around $200-300 for 8hrs/1 evening.

Not only will you get hands on training easily worth the cost, but you will get to put your hands on a variety of lights. Shooting students love to show off their gear; you can sample a variety of light brands during use without investing money into lights you only handled in a store.

Why do you also need a utility light if you have a 200 lumen combat light? Because combat lights eat up batteries like fat kids eat cake. And you do not need that much light to track a wounded deer or look at a map.

A good utility light will run a long time on lithium batteries. Angle-head military lights and Mini-Mags give you a lot of bang for your cash. A head-lamp, like the ones made by Petzl, are even better. Once you have a decent headlamp, you may just write off other utility lights entirely.

If you like a tiny light, Coast makes lights the size of a bullet that will run off watch batteries. My first Coast light lasted over 5 years before the first battery change. These little rockets are great key chain lights.

Also consider lights made by Lazer Brite. They run on batteries like the ones in your key fob, and are not much bigger than a

conventional chemlight. They are threaded so
you can combine several together. They come
in a variety of colors and they come in IR too.
In my old unit we carried these lights during
PT; using mine for an hour a day, 5 days a
week, the original batteries lasted 3 years.

What about renewable light?
Department stores sell solar "yard lights" that
are meant to be placed on the lawn, for $1-$15
each. They fully recharge on a sunny day. Most
have an on/off switch. During a major power
outage, you can charge these during the day
and bring them inside at night for lighting.
They are good for the outdoors too. They are
lightweight and stow easy in a pack. Just stick
one in the ground by your camp site in case you
need more light than the campfire to work with
after sunset.

14. Communication

Communication often ends up as an afterthought unless you have ever been caught completely without it. We take our gadgets for granted. We have become accustomed to talking to people or listening to people around the planet in almost instant time. Hell, we even casually browse through photos sent back from the edge of the solar system. All that data travels on a fragile web though.

A good emergency plan implements basic communication equipment in case the normal communication networks are out of service. It does not matter "the why", but just imagine all the satellites are dead, the World Wide Web is offline, and the phone lines are silent. Or imagine your state has an information blackout in concurrence with other infrastructure failures.

It does not matter why right this second, but your ability to call from work to the house is gone. You cannot email, social network, text, or anything. Your cell phone and computer just became expensive night lights. Whatever you have not already coordinated at this point is moot, because you cannot yell ten miles away with your voice.

Having an ability to communicate off the network really comes down to two things. The first is situation awareness. I need to know what is going on out there. The second is ability to coordinating teamwork, because without two-way communication we are all alone.

Situational Awareness: Situational awareness can be as simple as a police scanner. Almost everywhere the dispatch channels for Fire/EMS/Police is unsecure. (Some areas have secure channels for some calls, but the main dispatch is not encrypted.) You can hear what is unfolding nearby in real time. This could give you a jump on a problem or at least provide you with important information.

Having a portable AM/FM/Shortwave receiver is great too. I am amazed how many people do not own these. They fit in your hand and cost $30. The idea is to be able to gather information to make informed decisions.

Another part of situational awareness is knowing what is available for everyone else to talk on in your area. Almost everyone can quickly find a CB radio. Also, countless people have the small hand-held short range radio sets made by Motorola, Uniden, Garmin, Cobra etc. Regardless who makes the hand-helds they can talk to other brands.

Why would I monitor and scan CB nets and the little hand-held nets? I have two great reasons. First, I may need to know who is nearby in case I decide to contact them. Second, I want to hear if a group of wannabe marauders is snooping in my area. A vehicle mounted CB has a range of about 2-5 miles, a CB walkie-talkie has a range of about 1 mile, and hand-helds reach $1/4^{th}$ to 1/2 a mile (400-800m). (Yes I know some advertise 20 to 50 miles, but that is horse poop.) So if I pick up people talking, they are local—maybe really local!

The bottom line is monitor whatever you can, when you can. It may save your life.

Electronic War: Any radio signal device can be monitored and tracked. If it is digital it can also be remote operated.

Civilian GPS runs on unencrypted signals. To avoid being tracked, remove the batteries until you need it; immediately remove the batteries when done. Avoid using it unless you absolutely must verify your position. GPS is also subject to local jamming. GPS can only work if it can talk to satellites. One way to tell if a major war is imminent is the commercial satellites will start to disappear from your GPS tracker; the satellites are being turned off and shot down.

Cell phones are just digital radios. Your phone can be used to track you. It can be remote activated to passively listen and record images. Smart phones imbed large amounts of data in texts, photos, etc also.

Jamming- Any signal can be jammed. All you need is a powerful transmitter on the same spectrum to blast a stronger signal. Proximity and strength of signal are the key factors. Imagine you are in a room talking to other people and a man walks in with a megaphone and starts yelling so loud that nobody else in the room can hear anything but the megaphone. That is jamming. Your options are to 1. Destroy the jammer 2. Get a bigger megaphone 3. Switch communication method 4. Relocate away from the jammer.

False-Indicator- Any signal device (2-way radio, GPS, phone, smart watch) can be used to track someone. It can also be used to falsely indicate a position. If you are being tracked by phone, switch phones with somebody. Or leave your GPS behind. The device is being tracked; not you. If you know this you can utilize it to deceive.

Deception- Unsecure radios, like CB, Maritime, etc, can be used to deceive threats with misinformation. If you suspect you are being monitored, you can throw off your enemy with fake information about your activities, numbers, strength, weapons, or anything that you decide. You can send the enemy on a wild goose chase or set him up for an ambush.

Two-Way Radio Communication:

NOTE: We will not discuss HAM radio, MARS, or Shortwave radio here. If you want to get that up and running it is a few more books.

NOTE: We will not discuss modern military radios. You cannot get them anyway. Even if you did get one, the encryption changes frequently and you will just have a paperweight. When used in plain-text-single-channel mode (non-encrypted) all you have is a radio more powerful than the FCC allows that operates in the UHF spectrum. Military radios also require unique and uncommon wires and adapters to connect to antennas and power.

NOTE: We will not cover police/EMS radios. These cost several thousand dollars each and are under the same FCC rules as a radio in a department store. The reason these radios have so much range is all over town and along the highways there are "repeaters" placed on towers and buildings which send every transmission along the repeater network. If repeaters go down, these radios have very limited range. I learned this from using M/A-COM P7100 radios on base security; if the repeaters went down, you have to switch to cell phones to reach anybody.

Handheld- Some folks call them "bug out radios". For survival purposes, the most practical models are made by Motorola, Uniden, Garmin, Cobra etc. They are sold in pairs or sets of four and some are rechargeable. They fit in your palm, are very lightweight, run on very common AA batteries, and have a range good enough for use on a farm or ½ mile square area.

I tend to stick with Motorola and have around 16 of them for emergency use. I frequently let the kids take a pair out to play with; it keeps them familiar with their use.

A short piece of 550-cord will secure these little radios to your vest or kit so you can just push a button and speak as needed without moving your head. Rain will interfere with the microphone, but it is an easy fix. For wet weather, we tape a sandwich bag over the radio. Many folks pop the "call" button off of them because accidently hitting the call button will cause every radio to "ring", which can compromise everyone's positions.

Note that these little radios will not work on the CB or marine bands. If you want hand-held communication with a CB base station, vehicle, boat, etc, then you move up to slightly larger radios. For that purpose, I recommend radios like Cobra HH 38 WX ST or a Uniden Atlantis 250 VHF. Check out those radios to get an idea what features will serve you.

Fixed-Mount- This puts you in the class of CB/VHF. The good news is you can transmit further, since you have a bigger antenna. The bad news is the more distance you transmit, the more careful you should be.

A rule of thumb is that a great radio with a poor antenna will get mediocre performance, while a mediocre radio with a great antenna will get good performance. So if you get the top-of-the-line radio, put in the effort to get the right antenna and tune it.

A radio like ICOM IC-M412 or Uniden UM380 will mount to anything from a 4-wheeler, car, truck, boat, or can be powered in your house as a base. While hand-helds run on 4 or 5 watts, these fixed radios push out 25 watts. Combine these with good tall antennas and you have some communication range in the class of military field radios.

Telephone Communication: Land line phones have a lot of merits, especially for survival retreats. I am not talking about the phone company lines, but homemade closed loop lines. They run on little or no power, cannot be jammed, and are impossible to monitor unless somebody taps directly to a line. Unlike a radio, land lines are very secure if well hidden. The only downsides are that these devices are stationary and if someone finds your wire they can follow it back to you.

A closed phone loop can do several things: have contact from a command post to guard post/s; communicate between observation/listening posts; connect a neighborhood or small community; the imagination is the only limit.

The easiest way to accomplish this is to buy surplus US military TA-312 or TA-1 field phones, or a combination of the two types. You can connect them with military commo wire or common speaker wire. My first few years in the army, we used these phones extensively. A TA-1 runs with no external power supply; you just push the button a few times and an electrode inside sends enough juice over the wire to ring all the phones in the loop. You can talk with these for 1-3 miles, depending how dry the wire stays. The TA-312 runs on D-cell batteries and is good to talk for several miles. Battery economy is surprisingly good. Both types, TA-1 and 312, will work on the same loop, or you can switchboard them to individual lines.

If you are willing to experiment a little and do some tinkering, common house phones can be cheaply converted to closed loop systems or "party lines". The hardest part is making a low voltage system to trip the ringers.

Visual Communication: Why do I mention this? Because outside of the military, I have not seen any groups put any serious effort into this. Everything from hand signals to pre-established color codes become vital if other communication methods fail, become compromised, or are undesirable. Once you are jammed, monitored, or a radio breaks, it is too late to establish a signal code on the fly.

A red chemlight or bandana can indicate a casualty. Green can mean no casualty. A strobe light (IR strobe if you have NVG's) can signal position. Yellow smoke can indicate cease-fire or break contact.

Flare guns are cheap and easy to use. A flare from home base can indicate to rally. Or a flare fired at a point can tell everyone to focus fire in that area. Rifle tracer bullets are good for this too.

The sky is the limit. The point is, have it established sooner than later!

Sign/Counter-Sign: This is used to tell friend from enemy. Numbers are the easiest to use.

Let us say we are going to do a night linkup. Our sign number is 5. As I approach, I blink a light or tap on metal 3 times. Your reply would be 2 blinks or taps. If our sign number was 7, then your reply is 4. No matter the initial number of blinks, the reply equals our sign number.

This system can be used with anything from radios to knocking on doors.

Let us say during an emergency we are scattered in a dark building with enemy also inside. Our sign number is 5. I hear movement against the wall and think it is you. I tap the wall 2 times. Your reply tap is 3. If you do not reply or reply wrong, then I know to open fire. A very strong point of this system is voices are not used. That is important later so that an enemy cannot identify you by your voice.

This system works for "proof of life". Let us say a rival group has kidnapped one of our members and wants to exchange them for food. How do I know my person was not killed during the kidnapping? I ask for proof of life. If our sign number is 8, then I can send the number 6 and wait for a response of 2. At least I know if I am bargaining for a breathing person.

Panic Code: This is a covert way of alerting friendly people that an enemy has seized control.

Let us say home base is captured for the purpose of ambushing a returning patrol. During radio check-in the captors must let a person on home radio reply or the jig is up. (Same scenario can happen over a routine cell phone call.) Our panic code is "Tomato" + a number. Let us say home reply is, "Good to hear you. We've been waiting on you to bring home the 4 tomato baskets." That tells the patrol there are 4 enemies in the house. Or they might say, "We hope you brought back a bunch of tomatoes." That means there are an unknown number of enemies.

15. Hot/Cold Weather

It is not hard to underestimate the affects of hot or cold weather when most of us live and work in controlled climates. The modern miracle of air conditioning and central heat mostly keeps us separated from the brunt of summer and winter. But during a catastrophe this luxury is one of the first things to go away. Even if you find a way to maintain such a thing, it will cost you an enormous amount of resources and may ultimately become unsustainable.

This is not just a matter of being comfortable or being tough. This is about multiplying your odds by protecting your health and stamina. If you are surviving a disaster level event, most things in your life are severely out of your control; *that is why it is a disaster*. So, whatever you can put in your favor, you must do so.

Being unprepared for hot or cold weather, or even wet weather, is a guaranteed way to lower your stamina, waste energy, reduce productivity, lessen alertness and judgment, and become more vulnerable to infections.

Hot Weather- Anything over 80°F (27°C) goes into the realm of hot weather. This may not sound like much, but if you throw on a hiking pack and start a 5 mile walk you will quickly realize it is hot. The effects on your body will multiply exponentially as every degree of heat increases.

Heat kills people every day somewhere. Even in places where people can call 911 and be at a hospital in minutes, underestimating the danger of heat kills and mentally cripples healthy people. I emphasize that it happens every day. So just imagine the threat when there is no 911 or a hospital to help you. Letting yourself become a heat casualty during a disaster level event is likely a death sentence.

The effects of heat are cumulative on your body. If you expose yourself to heat constantly, without rest and proper food, your body will not recover. Every minute that goes by will make you more susceptible to injury. I saw this firsthand in Iraq, where during a week-long battle during August we evacuated ten heat stroke victims for every one person with combat trauma. It is vital during extreme heat to get a minimum of 8 hours of rest every night and take days off occasionally until you acclimatize to your conditions.

Illness and bad habits help this viscous accumulation keep cycling. Introduce cold, fever, alcohol, nicotine, drugs, caffeine, insomnia, etc and your risk increases.

Prevention! Prevention! Prevention!

<u>Heat Injuries</u>- Knowing these may save your life.

- Heat Cramps- Once your body is low on water and salt (electrolytes) you will experience painful cramps in your stomach. It will feel like you are going to have diarrhea, but if you try to shit you will feel constipated. Most likely your urine will be very dark. Lack of water intake, lack of food, and lack of rest/sleep cumulate to cause this just as much as heat exposure does. (My first personal experience with heat cramps was in the snow!) Once you have heat cramps, which can occur at any time, your stamina is reduced by at least 25% and your mental judgment is badly impaired. You are in a dangerous situation! Treatment: Go rest in the shade, preferably in the breeze. Loosen clothing and put a damp rag around the neck. Drink water and eat a small meal. Consider drinking a sports drink with electrolytes i.e. Gatorade, PowerAde, or hydration powder mix.

- Heat Exhaustion: This injury happens after the stage of cramps, but under some conditions you can exert yourself to heat exhaustion too quickly to notice the cramps. You will experience heavy sweating, weakness, dizziness, nausea, increased heartbeat, paleness, fatigue, and may faint. Your mental state will be confusion and you are not capable of good decisions. You are helpless and probably minutes away from stroke if not treated. Treatment: Move to a shaded area. Remove unnecessary clothing. Fan victim and sprinkle with cool water. Keep a cool wet cloth around the neck. If conscious, provide cool drink. Once nausea ends, eat a small meal. If unconscious, provide a saline IV. Should rest in cool place for 24 hours with 3 meals.

- Heat Stroke: Your body has lost so much electrolytes that you can no longer metabolize water or cool your core temperature. You stop sweating. The blood in your brain is starting to gel and stops flowing. Without intensive professional medical care, death is almost certain. Treatment: Move to shade and remove all clothing. Bed sheets or cloth dipped in ice water should be put around the neck, in the groin, under the armpits, and on the head. Core temperature will be 104-106°F. Introduce saline IV. Get victim to a doctor!

Clothing- Protect your head as much as you can during the day. Use whatever you must. If all you have is a handkerchief, or torn cloth, then cover your head. Preferably, wear a hat. A baseball hat is mediocre. A boonie hat or "cowboy" hat that protects your neck and ears is the best. Do not worry about fashion; staying alive is your style.

Note: Body armor and/or ballistic helmet will affect your body like a 10°F increase in air temperature. Wearing an NBC suit (CBRN suit) is another 10°F.

Neckerchiefs are great to have, so keep several per person during any season. These things are cheap, come in every color, and have a million survival uses. They can do everything from filter water, dust cover, be a tourniquet, a sling, bandage, pouch, signal flag, belt, insect net, etc. Relevant to hot weather, neckerchiefs help in many other ways. Aside from using one to protect your airway from dust, you can also soak one in water and keep around your neck. The evaporating water cools you while the cloth protects your neck from the sun.

Not meant to replace the neckerchief completely, but for $20 USD a Recon Wrap made by Spec-Ops is also very handy. It is made of lightweight synthetic material and can be converted into around a dozen garments. It can be a wet neck wrap, safari hat shade, etc. They come in several colors and are useful in any season.

Shemaghs can keep your head, neck, and shoulders cool. These are a roughly 40" x 40" (101x101cm) square piece of cloth that originated in the Middle East and was traditionally red, black, white, blue, or some combination. Over time they have gotten pretty common with US military and are now sold in subdued "tactical" color patterns of green or tan. They are practical and can be used like a giant neckerchief. In hot weather, you wrap it over your head so that it hangs loosely over the neck, shielding you from the sun.

Do not overlook sunglasses. They protect your eyes from a lot more than UV rays.

Even in summer, a thin pair of leather palm/full finger gloves is indispensable. A small hand injury can leave you helpless in an emergency. Imagine if you fall and get a handful of glass shards, or grab a hot rifle barrel and get instant 2nd/3rd degree burns. And you probably cannot just go get a tetanus shot if you cut your hand during a severe disaster. Protect your digits.

Your T-shirt is a simple garment that gets taken for granted. The T-shirt protects your skin and keeps you cool if made of the right blend. It is a comfortable barrier between

a durable outer garment and your skin. Failure
to use a clean T-shirt can result in sores and
abrasions from pack straps and kit that rubs
your body salt into your pores. I avoid 100%
cotton T-shirts for serious stuff. All that cotton
retains your sweat and stops "breathing" during
the day, and then during the night the sweat
chills your skin. A poly blend, like 50/50 or
65/35 poly and cotton is much better. You get
some of the comfort of cotton, but the poly
quickly wicks sweat away to evaporate.

Years of working in the hottest places
on Earth taught me to avoid underwear in the
heat. Underwear trap heat in your groin and in
humid weather can cause jock itch fungus/yeast
to grow. Cotton underwear is horrible. The
damp cotton swells and chafes your skin. If you
insist on underwear, try something synthetic
like bicycle shorts and wash them frequently.
(Foot powder in underwear can reduce chafing
and jock itch too.)

Your outer shirt does four things.
Protects you from hot sun rays; protects you
from insects, plants, and general scrapes;
provides pockets; and helps you blend in to
terrain (if necessary). It seems counterintuitive
to wear long sleeves in the heat, but it really is
better. Direct sunlight can burn you. And a

scratch on your forearm you might not think twice about now could become badly infected in a world where you are not showering. Material should be sturdy cotton twill like what BDU's or ACU's are made of, or a good 65/35 poly cotton blend. If not, find a close equivalent. You may find it a bad idea to run around in BDU's looking like a militia-ninja, depending on your situation, and not want that attention. In that case consider 5.11 or Blackhawk shirts; they are tough and functional without the camo patterns or full military look. For function with even less "tactical" appearance, the Cabela's Safari line very good. If money is an issue, Faded Glory makes men's shirts that can serve the same purpose for a bargain.

Avoid wearing shorts. A good pair of pants is the way to go. Blue jeans are okay, but not the best. If you do not mind looking like a lost paratrooper, military BDU/ACU style pants are very functional and hold up well. If you want to appear as forgettable as possible, go with cargo pants or hiking pants. They are tough, breathable, have plenty pockets, and look very unassuming.

Leather belts are hot. In the heat, a nylon rigger-style belt is the way to go.

Your footwear needs to match your activity and the climate. You can do almost anything in a pair of high-quality combat boots, but not necessarily in tennis shoes. For example, you do not want to trek around the wilderness in sneakers. On the other hand, when you are hanging around the retreat/house, a pair of sneakers is better; it gives your feet a rest. Cowboy boots are good snake protection, but not so good for a long walk. Boots/footwear is covered more in Chapter 9.

If where you are is hot and humid, avoid the suede tan desert boots. They are not made to stay wet for very long and constant exposure to moisture wears out the leather too fast. If you are in a rain forest or jungle region, I do not believe desert boots could last more than a month or two of regular use. Kiwi and other companies make sealant that may slightly extend the life of suede boots, but the suede is going to still start rotting. Use the suede tan desert boots in places that are relatively dry. Regular smooth leather is best for wet or damp climates. And smooth leather can be treated with mink oil, kiwi, silicon, paraffin wax, beeswax, and other products to make it last much longer.

Insects- Bugs are more than annoying; with no professional healthcare system available and hygiene supplies limited they become a health hazard. The list of insects and the list of diseases or venoms they carry are too long to cover here. Even if not exposed to insect-borne diseases, some will leave you with open sores or welts that itch until you want to claw your skin off. Anything that opens your skin in a disaster scenario leaves you vulnerable to staph infections!

During a catastrophe, a tiny bug can leave you just as ineffective, helpless, or dead as a gunshot wound.

For perspective, here is the world numbers of people killed per year by creature:

- Shark- 10
- Hippo- 500
- Tapeworm- 2,000
- Tsetse fly- 10,000
- Rabid dog- 25,000
- Snake- 50,000
- Human- 475,000
- Mosquito- 725,000

Research the insect-borne diseases and treatments in your area, or anywhere you plan to go. Become familiar, if you are not already, with the insects in your region that will lay eggs in your skin, bite, sting, or use your skin for lunch.

For example: Where I live the main insect threats, in no certain order, are *brown recluse, black widow, ants, centipedes, scorpion species, wasps, killer bees, mosquitoes, ticks, and red bugs* (chiggers).

I divide these into Poisonous and Disease categories.

Poisonous bugs like spiders, wasps, scorpions, etc cannot generally be repelled by chemicals or natural concoctions. Most are not deadly, but their venom can cause dangerous allergic reactions and will cause pain. Your biggest defense is awareness, common sense, and protective clothing. Most poisonous bugs do not consider you part of their diet; they attack you out of pure defense. So, learn where they nest and avoid those places. If you know that wasps nest in the wheel wells of abandoned cars, you know to check there before you go bumping around in one. Before bedding, check for ants and clear the ground of spiders, centipedes, etc. Always wear the right clothes! Think about it: If you are out foraging and disturb a hornet nest, do you want to be wearing shorts or long pants?

Disease carrying bugs consider you to be part of their diet. Therefore they are harder to avoid because they come find you. Your best defense is repellant, netting, and proper clothes. I keep a good supply of DEET spray and lotion available. I also keep a lot of permethrin based products on hand to treat clothing. While DEET is okay to protect the skin, it does not last very long. Clothing treated in permethrin can repel insects for weeks. Putting fresh "dryer sheets" in pockets also helps; mosquitoes do not like the odor. Citronella candles are good for sleeping areas. Supposedly there are natural herb repellants, but unfortunately I have never found one I like.

Tips:

- Keep your screens repaired.
- Do not overlook the very young or elderly in your group.
- Always check and clear bedding.
- Sleep with netting. Wear a head net if necessary.
- Light colored clothing makes it easy to see ticks.

- Know where insects live/breed/nest and avoid them.
- Have bee sting kits. And snake bite kits.
- Have medication like Benadryl (allergy) and Ibuprofen (pain/swelling) on hand.
- Have some EpiPens (Epinephrine) on hand if you have members with severe allergies to insects.
- Disinfect bites.
- If possible, sleep above 25 feet (7.6m) from the ground where most insects will not fly. It is windier and cooler too.
- When you bed down, keep your boots and clothes off the floor/ground.
- A Gortex "bivvy cover" makes a great summer-weight bug-resistant sleeping bag.

Hydration- Most people hear "hydration" and think of simply drinking water. That is partially correct. Steadily drinking water is part of hydration no matter how hot or cold it is.

Hydration is actually three things: water, salt, and carbohydrates.

Consider that it is totally possible to die of dehydration with a belly full of water! If all you do is drink water, without eating food, at some point your body will not have the minerals or energy to metabolize the water.

How much water? In any desert, whether freezing in winter or during the baking summer, if you lay in the shade with 1 quart (0.94L) of water, and do not move, you will be dead in 24 hours without more water. Places that are hot and humid, you may last a little longer provided you are smart and do not use any energy. Even in an air conditioned room, without water you can die in 72 hours.

It is always vital to have a lot of water, multiple methods of carrying water, ways to purify water, and knowledge of how to find more water. Never forget that eating is part of the hydration process.

You can cheat a little by having hydration packets or sports drinks available. These already have some of the minerals and carbohydrates in them that you need. It is a way to make your water get you further if you are low on food.

Your chances of survival greatly increase if you are highly familiar with water sources in your region. Are there natural springs nearby? Where are all the water towers and water treatment stations? Do you know how the water system in your town/region works? What pollutants are present in the local surface lakes, rivers, and streams? How will an earthquake/tornado/hurricane affect the water supply?

The average person in an industrial nation uses 100 gallons of water a day. The much water you have stored is going to go fast.

Simple water purification is to just filter out sediment and kill microbes with heat or chemicals; or remove microbes entirely by filter. Letting water drain through a bucket full of crushed charcoal and sand, and then boiling it for 30 minutes, will make most water safe. Or use a commercial water filter designed to trap microbes. Camping stores sell portable filters that will purify most water you encounter.

What about bleach? It is good if it is new. Bleach has a shelf life that should be considered 1 year. In just 6 months it already loses 20% of its potency in a brand new unopened bottle. It is hard to stockpile bleach.

Also, the colder it is, the longer it takes the bleach to work.

Iodine is an alternative, but must be properly stored. Iodine can be accidently ruined by poor storage. Also, if anyone in your group has a thyroid defect, they cannot have iodine. Just like bleach, temperature effects the time iodine needs to work.

A better option may be UV rays. If your water is free of chemicals and sediments, you can make it drinkable by killing microbes with sunlight. A 16oz water bottle on top of a square meter of tinfoil (or mirror) will be free of microbes in 30 minutes of direct sunlight. If you do not have sunlight, you can use a UV light.

If chemical pollution is present, it gets more complicated. Some things like certain alcohols can be boiled out of the water in open pots because it evaporates at a lower temperature than water. Then again, if distilled, the alcohol will just flow into the evaporation tube and get right back in the water. Your only choice may be a commercial filter dedicated to removing specific chemicals.

Know what is in your local water and own the right gear to clean it!

My advice is to have multiple methods to clean the water. If you have the time and energy, there is nothing wrong with a 4-step redundant purification process for drinking/cooking water, and perhaps a less redundant process for wash water.

Always look at the wildlife. If the nearby animals are ill or dead, that is a bad sign. Or if no wildlife is ever in or around the water, then that may be bad too. If the water cannot even support a minnow or tadpole, I probably will not trust it until thoroughly purified.

Marauding for water? *This is a dead end plan.* People that are smart enough to get their own water are smart enough to kill you many times over. The fact that they have water, and you do not, already proves they are smarter.

Salt- At one time salt had more value by weight than gold. Roman soldiers were paid with salt. The word "salary" comes from salt. During the Civil War, the Confederate Army was severely slowed down by a lack of salt mines. Wars were fought even as late as the 20th Century for mineral rights where salt was present.

We take salt for granted because it is pennies per pound now, but imagine if the grocery stores were gone.

Wild game is generally very low on salt content. If you plan to live off the land, do not overlook a source of salt. Either stock up a lot of it or locate where the local salt deposits are. If you live near the sea, you can also boil off sea water for the sea salt.

During hot weather it is very hard to preserve fresh meat. You are either going to have to smoke it, can it, or have enough salt to dry store it.

Why not stock it while it is still cheap?

Cold Weather- Anything under 60°F (10°C) begins to be cold weather. When I left Northern Europe, I thought that I had already experienced the coldest nights of my life. Little did I know my coldest night was to be in Ft Benning, GA during August. It rained on us for 24 hours and all we had was our helmets, rifles, and canteens. I will never know what the temperature was that night, probably around 60°F, but I shivered worse than any night I had ever spent in the snow. It was truly miserable.

The cold is a physical enemy and a psychological enemy.

There is a reason nearly all of those "reality survival" TV shows are filmed during summer or in the tropics: None of those folks would last past the second day if it was cold. People will mentally shut down from the misery and pain of the cold. The less prepared you are for the cold, the quicker it will numb your desire to live.

Physically, cold weather slows you down, robs your strength, makes simple tasks difficult, and dulls your judgment. Think of it this way: To travel on foot in the winter, the weight of your gear/clothes doubles as opposed to summertime. Proper gear is imperative. If you have the wrong gloves, your fingers stop working. If you save money by buying cheap clothing and gear, it is most likely less warm and heavier than the good stuff.

Cold Injuries- Once again, knowing can save your life.

- Hypothermia: This kills people even in the summer, mostly because people are not prepared for even the slightest drop in temperature. Wet clothing is almost always a contributing factor. In the winter, overheating and sweating can cause hypothermia if you stay in the sweaty clothes. Hypothermia happens when your heat loss exceeds your heat production and your core temperature starts to drop. It begins with violent shivering that tapers off as the body runs out of energy. Mental ability rapidly decreases and judgment is impaired. Loss of minor dexterity increases to the point that the victim mumbles and stumbles, and finally loses motor control. Reaction time will be sluggish. The victim will be tired, drowsy, confused, have weak pulse and low blood pressure. Treatment: Get the person somewhere warm and dry. Dry clothes and blankets is the best medicine. A warm meal and warm non-alcoholic drink will help too. Try to warm the core before warming the extremities or you may cause cool blood to rush into the core, further dropping the core temperature.

- Frostbite: This happens when your skin tissue freezes. Frostbite comes from exposing skin to freezing air, reducing circulation to hands or feet, contact with cold metal/plastic, or contact with fuel/antifreeze/alcohol in the cold. Note: Fuel in cold weather can cause contact freeze injury to the skin! Frostbite is a crippling, painful injury. The frozen skin will be numb to the touch, will feel wooden, may tingle and blister, and will be painful if re-warmed. Treatment: Treat for hypothermia. Do not unfreeze the affected skin if it may get frozen again. Submerge in 98°F water. Do not rub the skin or expose to too much heat. Seek a doctor. In severe cases, such as blistering or changing color, infection is likely.
- Trench Foot: Just 12 hours standing in water colder than 60°F can cause trench foot. A severe case can leave you

helpless to walk. Your feet will go from numb to having hot shooting pain. Minor trench foot is swollen and red, possibly with bleeding, but becomes blue and pale as it gets severe. Walking will cause needle-like pain. Infection is very likely! Treatment: Get somewhere dry as soon as possible. Remove constrictive clothing. Wash feet with soap; dry thoroughly and cover in loose, dry cloth or socks. Do not rub, massage, expose to high heat, or pop blisters. Elevate affected areas. Seek a doctor.

- Chilblain: A combination of dampness and air below 50°F cause this to exposed skin. Cotton clothing can cause this to covered skin. With wind, it can happen as fast as 1 hour. The skin becomes swollen, itchy, red, and painful. Re-warming affected skin is painful and symptoms persist. Treatment: The affected skin must be kept warm and dry until symptoms cease.

- Chapping: This is not necessarily an injury, but may lead to discomfort, pain, and infection. It happens when cold and dry air displaces moisture from the skin. Exposure to sun and wind will expedite chapping. Common affected areas are the lips, cheeks, ears, and nose. Skin will become red and painful, and then may crack and bleed. Skin kept covered with garments or treated with lip balm or petroleum jelly usually will not chap. Treatment: Stop exposure to the weather. Cover affected area with dry cloth. Moisturize with lip balm or petroleum jelly.

The army taught me an acronym to prevent cold weather injuries that I will never be able to forget: COLD

C- Wear <u>clean</u> clothes. It may be hard to do, but dirty clothes do not insulate as well.

O- Do not <u>overheat</u>. Once you start to sweat, you are setting yourself up to freeze later.

L- Wear <u>layers</u> of <u>loose</u> clothing. It is easier to take off or add as required with layers.

D- Stay <u>dry</u>. Wet clothing will not insulate; you can also get ice next to your skin.

NOTE: Dehydration is still a major risk in cold weather. Do not lower your fluid intake just because you have not sweated. The cold air sucks the moisture from your skin and respirations faster than hot air; even if you are not sweating you are still losing fluid.

<u>Clothing</u>- Most of your heat escapes from your head, so it is important to keep your head insulated. A wool blend watch-cap works good, but a microfleece watch-cap (aka PT Cap) is even better. The synthetic fleece wicks away sweat and dries faster than natural fibers. The fleece caps also are very lightweight and fold very small, making it easy to have dry spares in your pocket. Several companies like Polar Tech, Tru-Spec, and 5.11 make quality caps.

NOTE: If you are going to be around fire or sparks, microfleece and polypropylene (aka poly-pro) may be a bad idea because it easily melts. Wool or Nomex® are much more resistant to heat and flames.

In extreme cold, a balaclava is a great idea. It covers the head, face, and neck. Most are made of wool, Nomex®, or microfleece. It can double as a neck gator.

The best neck gators are made of poly-pro or microfleece. These garments are very handy because it can be used in several ways. It can cover the neck, or be pulled up over the face and ears. A combination of watch-cap and neck gators is desirable because you can easily adjust on the move or when you stop to cool off or warm up. A Recon Wrap, made by Spec-Ops, comes in practical here too. It is a good neck gator on its own, or in extreme cold as a base layer under a thicker gator or balaclava.

Shemaghs can keep your head and neck warm also. These are a roughly 40" x 40" (101x101cm) square piece of cloth that originated in the Middle East and was traditionally red, black, white, blue, or some combination. Over time they have gotten pretty common with US military and are now sold in subdued "tactical" color patterns of green or tan. They are practical and can be used like a giant neckerchief. In the winter, use it like you would use a very big scarf.

NOTE: Several thin layers are better than one or two thick layers.

The layer next to your skin, the undergarments or "base layer", is extremely important. This is the layer that traps warm air on your skin but wicks away sweat before it chills you. DO NOT WEAR COTTON! Cotton will hold moisture on your skin and dries very slow. (Do not waste your money on cheap cotton "long johns" except for as pajamas.) For most climates, you want a very thin to medium, relatively tight, layer of soft material on your skin that pulls away sweat. Long underwear is usually the way to go. Either get a "silk weight" synthetic set, medium weight poly-pro, or a wool blend that has a polyester lining. Keep in mind that heavy-weight poly-pro long underwear is meant for some extreme cold. Generally, how thin or thick this layer should be depends more on your activity than the air temperature. If you are going to be walking or moving a lot, go for the thinnest. If your movement will be limited, maybe try medium. Only wear the heavy stuff if you are going to be still, or you will overheat without a doubt.

I generally keep all three types—thin, medium, heavy—in my winter bug out inventory, because I may use all three depending on if I transition from moving a lot to being stationary and vice versa. One day I may need to walk very far; the next I may spend in a hide position. The base layer can make or break you.

Your mid-layer goes over your undergarments. This layer should be of a medium weight and fairly loose. If you are going to be exerting yourself or if it is not very cold, this may even be your outer layer. Just keep in mind that if you get hot, you want it to be easy to remove. Common materials for this are wool, poly-pro, polyester, or fleece. Military poly-pro, "waffle" top/bottom, or Under Armour cold gear work well for this.

The insulation layer goes over the mid-layer and makes a thick barrier between you and the cold. This layer is best used to keep the core area warm. It may consist of a jacket or even a vest. Wool or synthetic fiber both excel for this job. If you want a fast drying, compact, lightweight insulation garment, I highly recommend US Army field jacket liners. The black fleece military liners are excellent too. In extreme cold, and when stationary, it is common to have upper and lower insulation layers, and even to have double layers.

Your outer layer should be thought of as your "shell". Factor in if you need it to repel wind or rain. Your shell generally falls in two categories; either water resistant or waterproof. Water resistant is something breathable, but sheds light moisture. Gortex or nylon is good for this. Waterproof is a shell treated to not absorb any water at all. Be advised that waterproof will trap in your sweat vapors.

If all the layering is too complicated, and you have the money, you can cheat because the US military already did the thinking for you. Buy yourself a 2nd or 3rd generation Extended Cold Weather Clothing System (ECWCS). It has everything you need for just about any cold climate.

Gloves are one area that I avoid synthetic material. If you have to touch something hot, you want leather and wool. Synthetics will melt to your hand. I like to keep several thin wool glove inserts too. If your hands get wet, just swap on dry inserts.

My experience taught me that thin boots dry faster than heavy insulated boots and it is easier to swap on dry socks than wait on heavy boots to dry. For that reason, I wear lightweight boots even in winter, but I wear thicker socks. A thin moisture-wicking sock under a heavy wool blend sock is as good as it gets. And by heavy, I mean thick. I only put on insulated boots if I am going to be completely stationary most of the time.

Do not neglect your boots. Leaving damp mud on them can let mold grow and accelerates rot. Dried mud pulls the oils out of the leather and causes it to crack. Clean your boots often and periodically apply a conditioner to the leather. I recommend natural products based with beeswax or mink oil. Such products keep the leather too soft to crack, and since water cannot get in the leather it does not rot. Silicon conditioner is a great sealant but does not penetrate the leather like natural conditioner.

Do not overlook wet weather gear. The best stuff is military surplus or gear made for waterfowl hunting. If money is an issue, go to the dollar store and buy several of the $1 ponchos. Even though I have state-of-the-art wet weather gear, I still keep several of the $1 ponchos in my vehicles and bug-out kits.

Towels get neglected for winter gear, but you need one or two to dry off if you get wet or sweaty. I pack microfiber towels because they dry fast and roll up very small. They are marketed as field towels, camp towels, or travel towels. I recommend getting either the L or XL sizes if you intend to use them to dry your whole body. The medium is only big enough for shaving and such.

Sleep Gear- Contrary to what most people think, it is not the air that steals your heat while you sleep as much as it is the ground. Therefore, always insulate yourself from the ground. I do this by always having either a foam sleep mat (aka puss pad) or a military style self-inflating sleep pad on my bug-out bags or in my bed rolls. Most camping stores or surplus stores sell these and they are worth it.

One item I NEVER leave out of my sleeping gear is an army poncho liner. It is most likely the best thing the military ever invented. It dries fast, weights ounces, can be stuffed into a cargo pocket, can supplement any sleeping bag, and by itself it is pretty damn warm. Roll one up inside two ponchos with a sleep pad and you have a portable bedroom warm enough for down to 45°F.

For really cold weather, do not risk your life with cheap sleeping bags. Buy a real "sleep system". If you have the money, get an army modular sleep system. If you cannot afford that, look at one so you can compare what right looks like when you go shopping for something similar.

Have bungee cords in your sleeping kit. When it is cold as hell and dark, you do not want to struggle with numb fingers trying to tie a poncho or tarp over your bed. Bungee cords instantly fasten and firmly hold your roof/windbreak up.

If modular sleep systems are not your style, and you prefer wool blankets, check out army surplus, Harbor Freight, or Northern Tool for bargain wool blend. If money is no issue, check out Hudson Bay, Woolrich, or Cabela's.

Emergency blankets or "space blankets" are okay as a last resort, but do not depend on them. Anyone that thinks you can actually get warm in those things has never tried it.

16. Camouflage

Camouflage (camo) means using *anything available* to conceal a person or thing. When you hear the word "camo" you probably think of military or hunting clothes. However, that is just one tiny aspect of concealing something or someone. To be effective, we should think of camo as manipulating what observers perceive in order to prevent detection and to prevent being targeted and attacked.

General: What the enemy sees is not what he is looking at and what he hears is not what he is listening to. That is camouflage!

Several key aspects of camouflage (CLLTDD "Clit-D"):

- Culture
- Location
- Light/Noise
- Timing
- Decoy
- Dispersal

Culture: Why would you worry about culture as a consideration for hiding? Because you are hiding from people, it will pay off to factor in their strengths, weaknesses, habits, training, experience, preconceptions, prejudices, etc. For example: Concealing your survival retreat from urbanite city-dwelling refugees is easier than hiding it from elite military, police, backwoodsmen, and so forth. A deterrent to a hungry refugee may just serve as an indication for a seasoned troop or backwoodsman.

An extreme example of this is how you may hide an emergency backup bug-out vehicle on your property. Let us say you hide a brand new 4x4 SUV in the bushes with camo netting. How would an urbanite city-dweller refugee react to stumbling upon it as opposed to an elite group of rogue troops? The refugee may be desperate or brave enough to bust the glass to search inside, but that is about all. If he had any sense at all he would go the other way rather than tangle with well equipped people hiding new SUV's in the bushes. Elite troops, on the contrary, just found solid evidence that they are very close to a big juicy target and they may begin more detailed searching and eventually raid you.

So for argument's sake let's flip how we hide the emergency backup bug-out vehicle.

Instead of a new SUV under camo netting, how about an old banged up SUV under some trees, with flat tires, the hood up, windows gone, no back seat, and no battery? Perhaps 100 yards away you have the battery, fuel, and a tire pump cached under the ground, or you have a wagon/cart at home to drag those items to the vehicle with. The refugee may sleep in the "abandoned" vehicle one night, and then move on. The elite troops will see a pile of junk and move on after a casual glance. But once put back in order, a banged up old 4x4 SUV is still as good to bug-out with as a pretty new 4x4 SUV.

The point is this: You need to consider "who" you are hiding from.

All of this applies to your clothing and bags too. How you dress can get you into trouble very fast. If you are in the middle of nowhere you can probably be okay dressed like a tacti-kool commando-ranger-ninja all day long. But getting yourself out of a city dressed like that will probably draw in attention you do not need. How is it going to go if you run into a police check point looking like SEAL Team 6-ish? Camouflage means "blending in"; not standing out.

The same thing goes for your gear. If you are walking up the turnpike with refugees and you are the only one with a 3,000cc Mt Everest mountaineering backpack or super tacti-kool Delta Force assault pack, it is not going to take long for: 1. A desperate person to target you for looking like you have what they need or 2. The police or military to target you for looking armed.

Walking out of a city as refugees flee, you want to look as bad off as they are. If your next two weeks of life support is in your bags, you want those bags to look like old school bags you found at the last second and packed at the last moment like everyone else. If everyone else is carrying stuff in plastic grocery bags, do some of that too.

Blending-in means looking the same as your surroundings. Humans see other people as part of their environment. Think of the other people as part of the terrain. You want to disguise yourself in order to not be detected as a source of food/water/etc.

Location: Part of this ties to cultural aspects, but it also literally means "where". Culturally, if you are in Maine do not dress like you are in a Texas honky-tonk; and if you are in Germany do not dress like you are in Hawaii, and etc and etc.

Anything you hide, whether it be a cache, a retreat, a vehicle, or whatever, always look at the big picture. Will a flash flood, tidal surge, earthquake, or any natural event keep me from getting to this thing? Is this a place that will become "high traffic" after a disaster? What are the reasons *this* location is an ideal spot?

Light/Noise: In general, when it comes to concealment, light is not your friend. Sunlight tends to illuminate objects and make them easier to define. Sunlight makes the slightest movement easy to perceive from far away. Light also makes you cast a shadow. You can be the exact color of the terrain, but your shadow makes you a highly visible dark spot that is easy to detect. Same thing goes for vehicles. A vehicle can be perfectly camouflaged, yet the shadow under it may as well be a "Here I Am" sign.

Dealing with light is done in two ways, preferably simultaneously. First, stay low to the ground as practically possible. Even if you are in vegetation, stay close to the ground. Second, try to stay in the shadows. Something that is under a shadow cannot cast a shadow. And shadows tend to conceal small movement that is detectable in sunlight. Even optics, like binoculars, cannot pierce shadows.

Noise is not your friend either. No matter how camouflaged you appear, you will be detected if you make noise. Your personal gear/weapon should not rattle. Your bug-out vehicle should not have loud aftermarket exhaust. Your retreat should be somewhat soundproofed (for normal noises like dishes rattling, kids playing, etc). Your boat should have an outdoor carpeted floor.

Timing: Things always change. Hiding anything must account for that fact in order to work.

If you hide it in the morning, double check it in the afternoon to see if the change in light direction makes it visible. This is especially true if you hide it at night. What about the seasons? A thing concealed during summer may be easily visible in winter.

What time will people be around where you are hiding? The very best way to avoid human detection is to avoid humans completely! If I know the local police and troops in the area implementing martial law do a changeover shift brief at 6pm that is when I will move about if I must. If I know the refugees stop moving from 12pm-4pm because of the heat, or in the early morning because it is cold, that is when I will move around.

Decoy: A decoy is just a thing that makes people look in the wrong place. This is an often overlooked option, but your imagination is the limit and someone cannot see you if they are not looking for you. Somebody cannot steal your food/water/fuel if they are trying to break into a fake storage.

I have seen decoys all around survival retreats. Fake guard dogs are one. Things like lights that come on several hundred yards from the house that throw off trespassers. Fake bunkers, fighting positions, and command posts are another one; fully rigged with sandbags, antennas, and commo wire; these decoys cause an attacker to waste time/energy/ammo assaulting nothing while exposing himself to real fighting positions.

The list includes fake food storage, fake fuel tanks, fake storage sheds, fake gardens, and fake vehicles. All these things are used to lure marauders away from the real stuff, which gives the survivalist time to react and implement the defense plan.

I have seen fake driveways that go nowhere. Fake lookout posts that would make trespassers have to bypass good terrain and negotiate dreadful terrain. And even fake windows and doors on structures to confuse attackers.

A decoy can be as easy as a sign. Would you enter a property that has "Biohazard" warnings posted on it, or enter a doorway with biohazard tape and stickers on it? This is especially effective if the disaster *is a biological outbreak*. You could even use chemical hazard warning stickers on water wells or food storage. For extra effect, place some body bags full of dirt in the shape of people beside the road.

A decoy that may divert some refugees for awhile is random signs on the road that say "REFUGEE CAMP #4. FOOD/SHELTER 10 MILES AHEAD" or "Refugee Shelter & Food, St Paul's Ministry, take next right and 12 miles on County Rd 1042. All Are Welcome." The point is whatever it takes to move them away before they find you and start looting.

Remember that two-way radios can be a decoy too. Anybody collecting data on your retreat or community can be deceived by your broadcasts. A carefully scripted psychological campaign can be more devastating than a bomb. Imagine for example that you are planning a raid on a survival community and you intercept CB traffic about a deadly virus outbreak among them, or some mysterious chemical or bacterial food/water contamination? Are you looking forward to the same painful death being mentioned on the radio? The psychological impact could devastate the enemy motivation/morale to raid your community and maybe even cause a fracture in the enemy leadership.

On the reverse side, a carefully scripted psychological campaign can be used to make a retreat with five people sound like a large, heavily armed, well defended community.

Dispersal: When working as a group, spread out some. It is much easier to see a glob of people, vehicles, or structures than it is to see individual people or things.

When camping, do not make the camp too tight. When you are parking a convoy spread around or across the terrain feature. When you halt on foot, push out as terrain dictates; a group of people to close together always slowly get the "campfire mentality" where they look inward too much and start talking too much.

Staying dispersed is also just good survivability! A group of people close together is much easier to focus one weapon/fire on in order to pin them down so as to maneuver against them with other weapons. When a group is well dispersed, the enemy field of fire must be bigger; this means he cannot focus one or two weapons, but is forced to use more to pin you down and deny you from moving. The bigger the enemy field of fire is (i.e. more dispersed you are) equals more time you have to fire back and maneuver.

Personal Camouflage: You may be thinking of jungle fatigues or hunting clothes, but let me reiterate that if you are in a big city, your urban camo should be to dress like the locals. Or at least until you get to somewhere more rural.

For the backwoods retreat or rural survival community, jungle fatigues or hunting clothes is not a bad idea really. At a minimum, natural/neutral colors that blend to the landscape are smart.

A few key points to staying undetected:

- Not being seen has more to do with what you do than what you wear.

- Staying motionless and out of sight is the best camo.
- No camo clothes can hide you if you move a lot in the open.
- Solid black is a bad camo concept, even at night.
- Old prison uniforms had black horizontal stripes because black is uncommon in nature and horizontal lines are even rarer. Vegetation grows vertical or upwards, not sideways.
- It is easier to make light clothes darker than to make dark clothes lighter.
- Shiny or reflective is bad.
- The human eye is conditioned to recognize the human form. The shape of your shoulders, your face, even your hand is detectable from far away by a human. The goal is to break up those shapes.

Hunting Clothes: There are really two types of hunting clothes: Cheap ones and expensive ones.

Places like Wal-Mart, K-Mart, Academy, and some online stores sell relatively affordable hunting clothes with a variety of patterns. These are usually imported from somewhere. If it is made in China or a place you never heard of, it likely is in this category. It is not a bad idea to have some of these types of clothes and sometimes you can find great deals on decent quality stuff. The good news is you can buy a lot of the "low price" hunting clothes. The bad news is not all of it will hold up very well. The dyes may fade very fast in the sun/rain/washing; the material will not stand up to much rough activity; and the stitching often just falls apart. I am not saying some cheap hunting clothes are not useful; I am just saying under harsh conditions it will not last long. If it seems flimsy in the store, try to imagine wearing it while you are trying to not get dead in a catastrophe with any foreseeable end not to be seen.

MidwayUSA, Natchez, Cabela's, Dicks, Bass Pro Shop are a few places to find high quality hunting clothes. The bad news is you have to pay for quality. The prices can be high, so look for discounts and bargain programs, especially in the off-seasons. Sometimes it is cheaper to buy winter stuff in the spring and summer stuff in the fall. The good news is it will perform mostly as advertised, hold up to abuse, last a long time, and is generally on par with genuine military gear. I learned a long time ago that for outdoor gear I would rather pay for high quality with dollars than pay for low quality with misery and pain. The good stuff is typically "Made in USA".

A good in-between store is The Sportsman's Guide. I find they have a mix of everything. To mention again, MidwayUSA sometimes does also.

What about the hunting camo patterns? Why are there so damn many patterns? Well first we must acknowledge the commercial aspect of the hunting industry. To make money they must make hunters think they are always on the cutting edge of the next thing. Some of the stuff is legit, but let's talk real; it is the same as selling fashion clothes to school girls, Harley motorcycle riders, Western aficionados, fitness enthusiasts, business executes, or anyone else. If nothing new comes out, the sales drop.

The affect of the hunting "fashion" industry means that you can probably find a pattern to perfectly match almost any terrain in your region. This sounds great right? It does until you discover that the hunting camo pattern that perfectly matches the 15 acres behind your house does not blend in good in any other 15 acres anywhere else within 25 miles. Unless your retreat is in a 100,000 acre evergreen National Forest, I would not buy a lot of evergreen-specific hunting clothes. Or if you do not live in the middle of endless hardwood forests, do not buy the entire newest super-extreme greatest highly advertised super-enhanced oak tree pattern in the store. Where I live you can walk 1 mile and pass through evergreens, hardwoods, grassland, limestone outcrops, and maybe some wetland/marsh. Most places are pretty much like that in their own way.

If you have a specific reason to buy a specific matched pattern, well that is one thing. Otherwise, if you are going to spend money on a new state-of-the-art camo pattern, my advice is buy the ones that blend in the biggest variety of terrain you can find.

Every rule has some exception, and the one to this is if you live where there are four seasons. Spring/summer camo patterns may perform dismally in fall or winter, and vice versa. In spring/summer, Mossy Oak and Realtree both make good patterns. For fall/winter, Cabela's outfitter and outfitter-brown deserve a good look.

<u>Military Clothes</u>: If you are going to buy military clothes, buy the genuine article or you will not benefit from it. Avoid cheap knockoffs because they will not last. Genuine US Military clothing will have a tag sewn inside with the contract name, a contract number, and maybe a LOT number. Sometimes it will have an NSN with 13 numbers that appear like 8415-01-519-9118 (the number varies by item but format does not vary).

The only non US contract I will recommend is made by Tru-Spec, 5.11, and Blackhawk. These companies make clothing/gear worn by the US military in combat, either from private individual purchase or local unit requisition, and it usually performs fantastic. Places to purchase include MidwayUSA, US Cavalry, AAFES, and Brigade QM.

Patterns:

Multicam- If there was only one pattern I could pick for anywhere on Earth, I would go with Multicam until I find something better. It has been around long enough to find on a variety of uniforms and gear. It is the closest thing I have seen to a truly "universal camo".

UCP - (Universal Camouflage Pattern)
Found on US ARMY ACU's, known as "ACU pattern". The last pattern I would choose for anything! It blends a little with some stuff, but a lot with nothing. Unless you are hiding on a gravel road it is useless. The grayish/greenish color is called "foliage green" but I have never seen any foliage remotely close to it. This universal camo pattern universally sucks. It has been around a while and is on all types of gear from packs to pouches, but I would not waste time with it. It is too green for desert and too grey for woodlands or grassland.

ABU- (Airman Battle Uniform pattern)
I do not know the name of the pattern but it is on the USAF ABU. It is pretty much as useless as the UCP. It is foliage green, but with tiger stripes. The pattern is unrealistic. Also, the genuine ABU only comes in winter weight cloth; good luck in the summer with that. It is available on a variety of gear but save your money.

NWU- (Navy Work Uniform pattern)
The original NWU Type I is a ridiculous blue digital pattern. It looks tacti-kool but is useless unless you are hiding from the most colorblind folks on the planet. The NWU Type II and III are actually very practical colors and pattern for

arid or temperate regions. They are worth consideration. Unfortunately, the patterns Type II/III are still new and not much gear is printed with it yet.

MARPAT- This is the USMC pattern and is available for desert or woodland. It is not meant to be a universal pattern like Multicam; instead it is more regional/climate specific like the old generation of DCU/BDU. My experience around MARPAT is it is a pretty functional pattern and works as intended. It has been out long enough to be available printed on some combat gear.

Woodland- This was the most common pattern of the BDU's. It is an okay pattern, but is generally too dark to blend very often. You can do a lot worse, but you can do better too. As soon as you transition from forest to pasture/grassland, the effectiveness of this pattern fails. Compared to something like Multicam, it is inferior.

3-Color Desert- This is a pretty good desert pattern. Maybe a bit too light for truly open deserts, like in the Persian Gulf, but for deserts like in the Western US it is reasonably effective. It can work in arid grasslands too.

5/6-Color Desert- This one is often called Chocolate Chip. It never did well in the wide open Persian Gulf terrain, but it is well suited to brushy and rocky desert terrain.

Tiger Stripe- This pattern just never goes away. If you are in some real triple canopy jungle or rain forest, it is a fair to good pattern. But anywhere else it has some problems. The inherent flaw is the stripes are going the wrong way! Notice that a real tiger has vertical stripes; because in nature there are almost no horizontal lines in foliage.

Every few years, some foreign surplus uniforms or copies hit the market:

CADPAT- This pattern inspired many other digital patterns like MARPAT and is used by the Canadian military and some US arctic units. It comes in arid, snow, and woodland. I saw this uniform up close in several environments and in my opinion it is very effective. The problem is that if you are not in the Canadian military, you cannot buy the real deal; instead you must settle for similar commercial versions.

DPM- This pattern deserves mention because it was in service with the UK for many decades and is highly copied and mimicked around the globe. It has been printed in a variety of shade variants from reddish to tan-like and many tints of green during its evolution. It has both woodland desert versions, with several evolution changes over time. When the woodland is printed in darker shades it suffers from the same thing as the old US woodland pattern did; it sort of blotched together instead of breaking up your shape. Overall it was a fairly effective pattern, thus its long service record. In the past decade the UK started evolving the DPM pattern and created a crossbreed pattern that looks like DPM was bred with Multicam. This is a very interesting pattern worth looking at, depending on where you intend to use it.

DPCU or AUSCAM- This turns up in surplus stores sometimes. It always makes me think of the camo you see in old duck hunting ads. It comes in a desert and woodland variant. Both are well suited for semi-open brushy terrain or semi-grassland. Note: The ADF is currently switching to Multicam.

Aspenflage- This one is a reddish Swiss pattern made of blotchy dots. It was used until a few decades ago by the mountain troops. It could blend well in some parts of the Alps obviously, but also in the Rockies.

Colors:

Coyote- Often called tan or brown, it really is not exactly either. It is one color that actually is honestly universal everywhere except on a polar ice cap. Because it is common in deserts, grassland, forests, and in the city, whether it is winter or summer, it makes a great color for things like web gear, ammo pouches, straps, slings, and bags. For clothes, it can work.

Black- Do not do it. It can catch the eye as quickly as white!

Tan/khaki- Pretty much too light for green places, but is better than blue or black. The advantage of combinations of tan or khaki is it does not look out of place in an urban situation, but can still effectively be used as camo in a pinch.

OD Green- It has been successfully used since WW1, so it must work a little bit. A green shirt and tan pants does not look like a commando uniform, but is a bit of camo if needed.

Uniforms:

There are so many uniforms it really deserves volumes, but I will talk about a few I am very highly familiar with.

As far as comfort and function goes, the regular BDU/DCU is not bad at all compared to other uniforms. It has plenty pockets and can be had in summer or winter weight. These days they are sold in a variety of patterns. In my opinion there is nothing wrong with the BDU uniform, if the pattern is right. It should get extra points for simplicity! These things flooded the market since being phased from service and prices on new ones are a bargain.

The ACU (which comes in several patterns too, including Multicam) is a bit much. The damn thing has buttons, Velcro, zipper, three different types of draw strings…and let me reemphasize a lot of Velcro. It is not simple. The general fit is not very comfortable. It has more than enough pockets though; the magazine pockets on the calves are a nice touch. The Velcro closers are loud and wear out annoyingly quickly; granted the army has deleted the Velcro on the cuffs and cargo pockets for simple buttons. For civilians, if you buy ACU's, immediately cut off the annoying useless Velcro on the outer arm pockets and the chest name/rank tapes. Is it a functional uniform? Yes, but you are paying extra for complicated stuff you do not need.

NOMEX coveralls can be highly comfortable, especially the old OD green ones. The advantage of NOMEX is it is flame resistant. If you may be exposed to flame, these are worth having. Consider them for vehicle operations. They make a decent base for a ghillie suit too, if you reinforce the elbows/knees.

FRACU's are made of NOMEX, but built like ACU's. They are slightly tougher and maybe a bit hotter, but if you may get exposed to fire, like in a crashed vehicle, they are the way to go.

Skin: Do not overlook your exposed skin. An un-camouflaged human hand may as well be a signal flag. And your face is visible for at least a hundred meters.

The practical way to camo your hands is to wear tan or green gloves. You can paint the back of your hands with skin paint, shoe polish, or soot, but this is a last resort. It is dirty. Gloves camo your hands while also protecting your digits!

The quick, sanitary, and efficient way to conceal your face is to pull a wrap, neckerchief, gator, or such up over your nose. If you insist on paint, just remember to darken the high points, like the nose, lips, ears, cheekbones. But lighten the low spots like the cheeks, neck, chin, etc. Remember the human eye is trained to recognize a face; your goal is to "turn the face inside out" by shading the high spots and lightening the low spots, thus confusing the observer's mind.

Weapon: Why camo a weapon? Well because it looks like a weapon. The human eye is skillful at detecting manmade objects that it recognizes from memory. You are carrying a one meter long black metal and plastic object like the one the enemy is carrying. Even if he does not see you, he may catch sight of that black rifle.

There are five practical methods to camo your bullet launcher: parts, tape, cloth, paint, or a combination of any of those.

Swapping parts is the most expensive method and is not possible with all types. All you are doing is swapping out all the furniture or stocks for pieces molded from earth-tone polymer like tan, green, or camo. Or you replace a black synthetic or wood stock with an earth-tone or camo stock. You turn a solid black weapon into one mixed up a bit with some natural colors. This breaks up the shape of the weapon to some degree. As far as cost effectiveness, this is the most expensive method but may give the least results.

Tape is the fastest and easiest method, at first. Find some camo tape and tape it up until the outline is broken up. The first problem with tape is that non-reflective camo tape is cloth. It absorbs the grease, sweat, grime, and dirt from daily carry and eventually turns black again. If you use tape, be prepared to keep re-taping. You must also frequently check for rust in humid climates. Gun oil commonly counteracts the adhesive on the tape, causing it to peel in some places. In fact, if you un-tape the weapon, the easy way to remove the glue residue is to wipe with oil or solvent.

Using cloth is the cheapest method; you can usually do it for free. There are two common methods to use cloth for this. The first is to sew a "sock" of camo cloth over the rifle forward of the receiver/magazine well. In the front you leave holes for the front sight assembly and muzzle. In the rear tuck the sock under the scope/optic if you have one. If the sock is scrunched, the crumpled shape breaks up the shape of the front of the weapon. The second method is to rip thin strips of camo cloth or painted burlap and randomly tie the strips on the weapon to give it a "leafy" appearance. A major advantage with cloth is it is easy to change based on location and season/weather. For example, if it snows just add some white strips. Drawbacks include the fact that you must frequently check for rust under the cloth, and you should not use cloth on a weapon they may get extremely hot. Weapons that are AK, SKS, Galil, or M14 styles, for just a few instances, have an exposed gas tube; if you rapid fire a few magazines, the cloth on a gas tube or block will smoke and may even ignite. Absolutely never use cloth on any machineguns either. The cloth method should be used on weapons that will only be applied for slow deliberate fire.

Paint takes the most time, but can be done to any firearm for low cost and lasts a long time. First, clean the weapon of any oil or grease. Next use masking tape to cover places you do not desire the paint; the ejection port, dust cover, optic lenses, dials/knobs, gas tubes, apertures, etc. Use a razor to CAREFULLY trim excess tape if necessary. Hang the weapon, muzzle down, from a wire or cord through the rear sling swivel. Thoroughly shake your spray paint. Krylon flat/non-glare is the best paint for this in a pinch. For more durability, get Duracoat. For yet even more, use Cerakote.

(Follow manufacturer's instructions! The following does not replace directions that come with any product.) Style 1: Add a couple thin coats of a base paint. Two thin coats last longer than one thick coat. Allow lots of time to dry in between. The base coat should be a light color like tan. Once satisfied the base coats are dry, you add at least two more colors with a thin brush. A medium brown and a medium green are good. Shape the green and brown like the vegetation where you are; whatever breaks the outline, but leave plenty of tan so the pattern has a 3-D affect. Style 2: Same technique for the base coat, except use a green that closely matches the color of vegetation. Once base coats are dry, you need a tan or very light brown spray paint. Lay pieces of vegetation, like pine needle boughs, fern leaves, etc against the weapon and lightly dust with the tan paint; alternate with light brown. This creates a 3-D affect. Tip: Practice your technique on an old newspaper before you do the weapon.

NOTE: Some of the Cerakote and Duracoat products, or similar, may require baking or curing. Read all the instructions first.

Vehicle/ATV/Boat: At some point you may need to hide your mode of transport. Good examples would be when you stop for the night, or perhaps if you must leave your vehicle to perform a task or errand on foot.

Obviously, your post-apocalypse survival vehicle should not be bright yellow or red. Go for colors like tan, dark green, brown, or gray. Of course in the case of cars/trucks/SUV, factory paint will be glossy clear-coat. An extra step would be to have the vehicle painted in a flat color or to install a "camo wrap/camo graphics" kit. Nevertheless, even if you make the vehicle body subdued, you still have reflective things like glass all over it.

No matter what color your vehicle, ATV, or boat is, it is recommended to cover it with camo netting or camo screen. The netting or screen covers the glass and interrupts the straight lines of the vehicle. If the net or screen is not lying directly on the vehicle it also disrupts the heat signature. Some folks stake down the net to prevent it from blowing away. I prefer a few randomly spaced bungee cords around the edges that quickly and silently secure the net or screen to whatever bushes or saplings are nearby. (Note: Do not roll up your net with bungees still attached. It will be a pain to unroll later as the hooks catch everything. Roll the net first, and then wrap the bungees around it.) If you park under trees, a couple bungees in the middle of the net are a swift way to raise the net off the vehicle.

Screen vs. net?

A camo screen is a fabric, like nylon or burlap, which is woven loosely in such a way that it is partially transparent, normally printed with a camo pattern on it. You ordinarily find screen in hunting stores and it is more likely to be a civilian/commercial item than a military piece. The advantage to screen is it is easy to maintain, durable, strong, and if nylon it lasts a long time. It can be used to improvise bed padding, hammocks, or blankets too. It is easy to cut large pieces to tailor fit objects. Screen is good for concealing things like ATV's, small boats, or snow mobiles. It is excellent for concealing small equipment also; just lay it over equipment and weight it down with rocks or logs. It does a decent job concealing things like utility boxes, air vents, or hatches to underground structures. It works fine to cover the windows of bunkers, guard posts, or to use as a hasty ground blind. The shortcoming of camo screen is it has minimal 3-D appearance at short range; it works better for observation from beyond 100m. It gives minimal concealment from devices that detect heat and does not disrupt ground radar.

Camo net is literally a net with other material fastened to it to give a 3-D appearance. It is based from military design. Early camo net was made by attaching strips of cloth in random patterns to large fish net. Modern net replaced the cloth strips with rubber or vinyl strips precut in long leafy patterns. The rubber or vinyl strips are fastened with plastic or metal clips. Genuine military netting uses aluminum clips, and this serves a second duty in that it clutters ground radar and to a small extent clutters heat detecting devices. You can add the aluminum to commercially sold netting, but unless you are hiding several vehicles nearby each other, it may not be a big concern. The benefit of netting is that when used as designed, it works great at almost any distance. In many environments you can walk right by camo net and not notice it. The disadvantage is netting is harder to maintain (although with a repair kit it is easy to fix). Your rubber or vinyl strips can easily get ripped off and in will dry rot if improperly stored. Netting snags a lot during setup/takedown, making it hard to put up a large piece with only one person.

At some point you may decide to convert a vehicle to a dedicated survival role. Along with camo you need to modify the lights. Consider a kill-switch for the tail/brake lights, or remove/cover the lights and housing. Do not forget to disable the cargo and dome lights, either by pulling the fuse or gluing down the door switches. Any unnecessary control lights, like the radio display or air controls, should be taped over. You can make blackout drive lights by covering 55-watt fog lights with blue plastic; this makes a dim light that lets you creep along a trail at 3-4 mph. For road travel, a single 55-watt fog light will let you roll along at 10-20 mph without lighting up the horizon with headlights.

17. Fire Ignition

You can find an everlasting source of clean water, you may even be able to locate sources of food that will feed you for the foreseeable future, but at many junctures you are going to have to create fire. Just like your collection of redundant methods to purify water or locate food, you need an array of fire starting methods.

NOTE: This chapter assumes you already know how to prepare tinder, kindling, and fuel for a conventional fire in a survival situation and know the burning properties of common wood/materials. This chapter assumes you already know how to prepare available resources (wood, coal, paper, etc) in wet/damp conditions. This chapter assumes you already know how to safely build fire pits or rings appropriate to the intended use (i.e. cooking, heat, light, forging, etc).

Primitive

These methods include the bow drill, hand drill, fire plough (plow), pump drill, stone combinations, and etc. These methods are called "primitive" for a reason. Another good word would be "obsolete". These methods are Prehistoric!

Is it good to learn how to do these things? Yes as an absolute last resort this type of thing could come in handy. I mean, if you have really let yourself get in one terrible pickle, I suppose you had better be pretty adept at this stuff. But be honest with yourself: If you legitimately need to use these methods to survive, you are not likely to last much longer, my friend.

All these methods are time intensive to get good at in a realistic scenario. It is one thing to do it in your garage. It is another thing to do it in the wilderness. You are not going to get good enough at this to matter by memorizing a book or article; you have to put in the hands-on time to become proficient at primitive techniques.

It takes a lot of energy to do this stuff. You will usually break a sweat. I have been in classes were a couple people got a fire going in 10 minutes while others took hours. The next day the people that took 10 minutes ended up taking hours. Primitive methods are not consistent. You simply cannot plan ahead and say, "It will take me X minutes and X effort to get that fire started."

You would not want to rely on primitive methods if you are injured, sick, exhausted, overheated, or have hypothermia. You may fail to start the fire even under pretty favorable conditions. Every little thing unfavorable to your circumstances pushes you further toward failure.

Archaic

Methods that are outdated (but not Prehistoric!) are good to have around as a backup plan. These techniques fall somewhere between "obsolete" and "inconvenient".

Two popular methods in this category are flint & steel and a fire piston. These were commonly used from early civilization up until the Industrial Age.

Most people know what flint & steel are. (When I say "flint & steel" I do not mean modern firesteel or ferro rods either. I mean an actual piece of flint stone and a steel or iron striker piece.) You simply strike a spark into a pile of fluffy fiber (tinder) and persuade the fiber to ignite with a little air. Dipping some of the fiber in gasoline or petroleum often helps out. Fibers are only limited by your imagination: pocket lint, hairball, fine steel wool, bird nest, fluffed cotton ball, abraded cloth, plant matter, and etc.

A fire piston works on the same principle that makes an aerosol can get cold as you spray or allow a diesel engine to combust with compression. Rapidly decreasing pressure while you increase volume makes something cold. Rapidly increasing pressure while you decrease volume makes something hot. A fire piston is simply a handheld tube that you push a piston down in. A hard push will create about 500°F in most fire pistons. So, you drop a piece of charcloth (charred cloth) or charred paper in the tube, push the piston in as hard as you can, remove the piston and dump the ignited ember into your fluffy tinder and coax it to burn, much like with flint & steel.

The disadvantage to archaic methods is two things. First, you must spend the extra time in preparation to get the best tinder you can without fail. You must also always carry around waterproofed tinder and charcloth. Unlike with modern ignition techniques where tender is not as critical, with these methods it is not negotiable. Second, if you injured your hand/arm/shoulder you will be really struggling to use these one-handed. Yes you can pump a fire piston one-handed, but you will have to open it with your teeth to get the ember out. If you lose dexterity in your fingers, either from burns or severe hypothermia or whatever injury, you can probably forget making this happen.

Are the archaic methods useless? No, because you can use these to save your matches or modern devices for real emergencies. These methods are also extremely renewable in the long run. If you live somewhere that flint is common, you can make fire indefinitely, long after matches are nowhere to be found. And a fire piston will last virtually forever; all you need is a source of pre-charred fiber, cloth, or paper.

Improvised

Improvised fire starting methods include water, ice, magnifying glass, batteries, firearms + cartridges, mechanical assisted friction, chemical combinations, pen flares, aerosol, and etc.

Should you learn these things? Absolutely, yes you should be aware because you just never know if you need to know it.

You should never consider improvised methods as a primary method of making fire though.

First of all, there is always a lot of luck involved. No matter how many strange unconventional ways you learn to create fire, you have to get lucky enough for the items you need to be obtainable first. For example: It is hard as hell to make fire with water if you cannot find any thin plastic wrap or perfectly clear bags. And how do you use water, ice, or glass to make fire if it is night, or just cloudy, or so windy you must stay inside? You cannot. You can pull a big magnifying glass that can burn a hole in metal from an old TV, but it is useless without sunlight. You cannot use a battery to make fire if they are all dead. You cannot use a power drill if you have no current. The list goes on.

Second, there is the danger. **Most improvised methods unleash an uncontrollable amount of energy in an unpredictable fashion.** That is why many improvised fire methods violate federal or state laws; read the labels on products or owner manuals with products and you will see the law stated sometimes. I must advise you to never practice improvised methods outside of a legally supervised class environment.

Messing around with electricity to spark a fire always presents some danger of burns, electrocution, and damaged equipment. The bigger the battery, the more there is the risk of injury. An electric arc can make a horrible burn and poisonous fumes. Lithium batteries also explode. Once, I saw someone damage a truck trying to ignite paper by arcing from the battery.

Using chemicals is just as dangerous. Knowing which pair of substances ignites on contact does not mean you know the correct amounts at the right temperature. A tiny miscalculation can make you instantly go from cold and hungry to agony and death. The fumes from such fire should always be considered poisonous.

Using firearms and/or ammo has always struck me as bad business. I have seen someone do it in 3 or 4 shots, but I have seen a person run out of ammo trying to do it too. One method is to pull a bullet from a cartridge and replace it with paper or cloth and fire it in the air, hoping to locate the smoldering paper in time to drop it on the tinder. Sounds good on paper, but it is hard to do in practice. It can work, but if you are injured and cannot walk all over the place looking for the smoldering paper, you may be screwed. If it is raining or windy you are certainly screwed. Dumping the powder into some tinder and igniting with a spark from flint & steel can work though. If you try to shoot a pile of powder, however, you will find that the hot gases from the muzzle blow the powder away before any muzzle flame reaches it.

Using power tools other than intended/designed to make sparks or friction heat should be obviously dangerous. Do a risk assessment. What may occur when I hit that button? Consider that the particles released in the air are harmful to breathe or if they get in your eye. The last thing you need in a survival scenario is a blinded eye, lost fingers, and a respiratory infection!

Pen flares and flare guns can work. You build the tinder and kindling so as to trap the flare and usually it will ignite from the heat. But once in awhile flares are harder to capture than you think and they ricochet out. Be careful! This is extremely dangerous and should not be practiced. It is not worth losing an eye, burning down property, or killing a bystander just to see if it works. It does work, but only do it to save your life.

Using aerosol is inherently dangerous. But if it is an emergency and you can create a spark from a flint, dead lighter, battery, or whatever, you can ignite most aerosols to make a jet of fire to light your tinder. Just take precautions and do not do it for the hell of it because sometimes the cans explode.

The advantages to improvised methods is that should you be lucky enough to find the right items, in the right conditions, and know exactly what to do safely, you may be able to start a fire without much more effort than normal fire starting procedures or methods. They key is to know how to do it, but do not go forth relying on luck. Hope is the weakest course of action.

Primary

Your primary methods should be SAFE, simple, reliable, small, and easy to use even if you are tired, sick, or have a broken arm in a sling. Having a variety on hand can save your life.

Butane Lighter- (Disposable) These are cheap and usually work. About 98% of the time, plain butane lighters do the trick. Disable the "child proof" feature and you can light it with one finger. I found that the most reliable design are the ones by BIC® and have flint ignition. These are easy to repair if they malfunction. I avoid electric ignition lighters (click sound) because if the igniter breaks, it is usually un-repairable. Shelf life of flint lighters is at least 10 years, as long as you store them in sealed dry containers so the flint cannot oxidize. Electric ignition lighters probably store indefinitely. It must be mentioned that extreme cold will affect disposable butane lighters. The colder it gets the less flame they make. They also may not ignite damp material. High altitude affects the quality if the flame too.

Matches- Regular stick matches (kitchen matches) should never be overlooked. I dip the tips of "strike anywhere" matches in candle wax and store them in pill bottles with a cotton ball, piece of steel wool, piece of sandpaper, and a chunk of starter (sawdust and wax mixture) or dry pine resin. For very little money, this creates waterproof matches in a waterproof kit that is easy to carry and can start a fire in damp weather.

Avoid paper matches for outdoor use. They are very cheap and great for lighting the wood stove, fire place, candles, and lanterns. However, no paper matches, not even the moisture resistant ones in MRE's, do very well in the weather. Not only that, but paper matches have a short burn time and get blown out easily. It can take several paper matches to ignite something that one stick match would ignite effortlessly.

Zippo- I put these awesome lighters in all my bug-out gear and carry one everywhere I go. Temperature or altitude does not affect these lighters and they are tough as hell to break. Yes they do dry out in improper storage, but who cares. In an emergency a Zippo will run on paint thinner, kerosene, ethanol, finger nail polish remover, gasoline (*be very careful with gasoline; it will flash and it can explode; emergency use only and use only a little*), diesel, JP-8, JP-4, sulfur free diesel, vodka, rum, rubbing alcohol, lamp oils, cologne, after shave, camp stove fuel, moonshine, and probably a lot of things I have not tried or seen.

Tip: *Under normal conditions only use approved lighter fluid.* If you must substitute approved fuel, aim for alcohol based fuel before petroleum based fuels. Alcohols burn cleaner, leave less soot, and are less likely to flash or explode. Less is more! The first time you try new fuel, try tiny amounts and move up until desired results.

Tip: NEVER strike a Zippo when it is not in its case; it will burn on both ends and be hard to extinguish. Always wipe excess fuel residue from the case before striking. Leaving the lid opened 10 seconds before striking prevents flashing.

Tip: A Zippo stored in a condom, rubber glove, or balloon tied shut will last a long time.

Tip: You can pack two or three tiny cotton balls in the Zippo, and use those as tinder if everything else is unsuitable.

An empty (dry) Zippo can be used to ignite small bits of tinder. Move the dry wick out of the way and insert a fluffy tinder into the cage. Strike the wheel until a spark catches. Gently blow on the cage until the tinder smolders, and then drop it in to your tinder pile and coax your fire.

If your BIC lighter runs out of fuel, the flint will work fine in a Zippo. Extra flints are cheap and easy to find too. I put extras in the bottom of the Zippo case. I also seal flints in wax and store them in airtight baggies for future use.

Ferro Rods- Any experienced survivalist likely has these rods somewhere. In the army I kept one about an inch long taped to my dog tags. They are manmade flint and come in sizes from the size of pencil lead to bigger than whole pencils. Your cigarette lighter basically has a ferro rod for a "flint".

You simply point the rod at a pile of tinder, place a knife spine edge/scraper on top of the rod, and draw the rod back against the knife spine/scraper and it throws sparks. A piece of rough, raspy metal produces the most sparks. It is better to use the rod with a dull scraper instead of a knife, to avoid accidentally cutting your hands. It may sound silly, but I have seen some people cut pretty seriously doing less.

The sparks are around 3,000°F (1,650°C) and will ignite a variety of material as long as the material is dry or lightly saturated with flammable liquid/gel/oil. The fluffier, more frayed, or more crumbled the material the better it works.

Constantly I hear outdoorsmen preaching the virtues of ferro rods as a backup fire ignition method, but I have always looked at it the other way around. I say use the rod when you can to save your other ignition tools.

Conserve your lighters and matches for when you are in a hurry, too tired, or too injured to fumble around with coaxing embers and such.

The real drawback to ferro rods is the need for dry tinder. If you forget to collect some as you go about daily business, or you get yourself drenched, you may not be able to utilize the rod the moment when you want to.

Another shortcoming is that ferro rods are very difficult to use with one hand. It can be done if you can step on the rod or otherwise pin it down to scrape it. However, if you have ever had a broken bone, dislocated shoulder, smashed hand, or comparable then you understand why I say this: In a survival scenario with those injury types I would just use the matches or my lighter.

Alternate (emergency)

What works in a routine situation may not work when things go to hell. Imagine that your family just fell in a stream during a blizzard at night, you pitched a hasty windbreak with a poncho and bungees in a stand of young pine trees, there is still wind and sleet pelting you all and you have about one minute left before you all succumb to hypothermia and die.

If you think you are going to ignite available tinder with a BIC or match, you are dead. If you think you will not be shaking so severely that you cannot properly pull together tinder and kindling, you are dead. If you try to build a fire with conventional methods, you are dead.

Right now you have to cheat as violently as you can. All you have time to do is snatch whatever kindling is within arm reach, put it in a pile, a light it with something that will boil out the water.

Emergency Tinder- Every member needs to have a pack of emergency tinder on them. Not tinder you use for routine fires. You need no shit emergency specially treated tinder that will ignite damp wood. It needs to be in a small waterproof container that you can open even if your fingers are numb.

My solution is a pair of tiny Rubbermaid rectangular bowls with easy-off lids (volume about 1.2 cups). They are kept in the top flap of my pack, sealed in a Ziploc bag. In both bowls I glue a strip of sandpaper and NATO waterproof matches (or camping storm-proof matches) under the lid. The reason being, the lid is a wind/rain shield so you can strike the match under cover.

Inside each bowl is my personal 2 layer concoction.

Bottom layer: Stir together 10% bacon grease or hot pine resin (Or 5% diesel/kerosene/BBQ lighter /etc) and 90% wax, and then mix in a generous combination of sawdust, shredded steel wool, and 550 cord guts. The bowl should not be over 2/3rd full. Let it cool until it hardens. Purpose: This will burn hot for several minutes. Bacon grease accelerates the wax; sawdust/steel wool adds heat; 550 cord guts burn a long time. Even the rubber bowl burns great. (If you do not like making concoctions, you can fill the bowl 2/3rd full of fire starter log. It is almost as good, but harder to ignite.)

Top layer: Slowly heat Vaseline until slightly melted, and then soak dryer lint (or cotton) until lightly saturated. Do not make the lint dripping wet; you want it moist but fluffy. Pack in the bowl over 1st layer until 4/5th full, keeping the lint fluffy so that air is trapped in the fiber to aid ignition. Do not fill to the brim. Push a hole in the center about ¼" x 1" or 5mm x 25mm with your thumb. Fill the hole with shaved magnesium (or crushed fuel tablets). Purpose: This top layer burns hot briefly to ignite the bottom layer. The hole filled with shaved magnesium will especially burn hot. Just a few sparks will ignite the magnesium.

CAUTION: These things are dangerous; they will ignite fast and burn very hot. Some splattering should be expected, especially if sleet/rain/snow hits the fire. Burning wax/plastic/grease may flow out of the fire. Avoid using in a confined space; fumes will be harmful. During hot weather, contents may melt and leak if not sealed.

Lantern Wicks- Another emergency kit that works great, but suited for places where you do not encounter blizzards, is made of lantern wicks. Simply cut the wicks (or cotton straps) in to strips about 4"-6" long and fray about 1" of an end and soak the other 2/3rd in hot wax. After the wax cools, place the wicks frayed end down in a waterproof can or bottle with an opening big enough to put your fingers in, and then soak the wicks liberally in Zippo-type lighter fluid. Place the cap on and wait 5 minutes for the wicks to absorb. Open the can and soak them again until there is some fluid in the bottom. Wax may dissolve some but is normal. Keep sealed and do not leave open. Putting tape around the lid gives extra sealant. In an emergency a tiny spark is enough to ignite the frayed end and the wax will add to the burn time. One or two strips will get wet kindling going.

Maybe you do not have the time or interest in concocting your own emergency tinder kit. You can buy commercial products that will do the trick in some emergencies. These products are great to have when conditions are just plain old wet also.

Starter logs- You can cut regular fireplace starter logs to size, wrap in news paper lightly soaked in BBQ lighter, and seal them in Ziploc bags for use in very wet or emergency situations. They usually do the trick. Camping and outdoors stores sell small starter logs especially for campfires. Be aware that the purpose of starter logs is to burn several minutes to get wet kindling burning. Starter logs DO NOT necessarily light very easy. A spark will never do the job. You must have a good flame to get the starter log to light. If you are in very windy and/or wet conditions, like in a sleet storm, a BIC or match will most likely not get a starter log to burn. A butane "torch light" may do it, if it does not fail because of the cold. Tip: One solution is to tape a small "road flare" or "highway flare" to each log when you pack them. If you need a fire while it is too nasty to light a match, a flare is easy to strike and will get the log going.

Fire Starter Products- Several companies make different starters for the camping market. Coghlan's makes waterproof fire sticks that come in 12 packs. They are small and easy to carry. Another high-quality item is made by Zippo and called Campfire Starter. It is a flat waffle made of cedar and wax, designed to be lit as is or broken into 4 pieces. You must have a flame to ignite it.

Magnesium- I have used magnesium since I was a kid. I keep a magnesium starter in all my kits, bags, etc. For $6 USD, you cannot beat the simple starter that Coghlan's makes. It is a 3" or 75mm long block of magnesium with a wet/dry striker on the back. Use your knife to shave a little pile of magnesium, and then slide your knife over the striker about 1" from the pile, and you get a 5,000°F fire for several seconds. Note: A magnesium starter is usually not enough to get wet kindling going, but it will get wet tinder to burn. Combine a magnesium starter with waterproof fire sticks or a starter log and you are probably good as long as you can protect the pile of shavings from the wind.

Caution: There is a danger of severely cutting yourself while applying these. The risk is even great when you are cold, tired, and in the dark.

Spark- A flint & steel or ferro rod kits are good, and should be used to save matches, but in an emergency you need to cheat. There is a striker called BlastMatch™ that throws sparks hot enough to ignite a t-shirt or such. It is 4" long and can be operated with one hand, which lets you use your free hand to shield the tinder from wind. You just push it against the surface where your tinder is and get hot sparks. Igniting pocket lint, steel wool, shredded fabric or leaves, fuel damp rags, magnesium, etc is no problem. I found mine for $18. The disadvantage of a BlastMatch is that if you are striking tinder on a soft surface, and you cannot find a rock or decent sized log, you are screwed unless you improvise with a large knife blade, ax head, or something you can ignite tinder on. The tip will just push into the mud, sand, snow, and so on otherwise. This devise will not take a lot of abuse either; it is just plastic. If you get carried away and break it, you basically now just have a ½" ferro rod. I save mine for emergencies.

As far as ferro rods, they can work in wet conditions if you do your part, and like doing things the hard way. Just do not try it as your first option in dangerous conditions or you may regret it. You can even manage to strike them one-handed if you can pin the rod down under a rock, your foot, knee, leg etc. A ferro rod kit worthy of mention is the Strikeforce. You can carry emergency tinder in the handle, which is a very good thing. It is pretty tough and small enough to ride easy in a cargo pocket.

Easy Flame- There is several emergency butane lighters on the marker. They go for $15-$80 depending. They are not bad to have, but never depend on one as your only emergency flame. They use electric ignition (piezoelectric), which cannot be repaired if it breaks, and run on finicky butane systems that are temperamental in the cold. I have had too many expensive butane devices fail to trust one in a dire situation.

Zippo makes an emergency fire kit that utilizes a wheel/flint system to ignite little water-resistant wax sticks that you then drop in whatever you are lighting. It is damn near fool proof and cost about $10. Speaking of Zippo's, a regular one is not affected by the things that make butane lighters break down.

Storm Matches- Many folks make their own waterproof matches by dipping strike anywhere matches in wax. This idea is decent and it does improve the match; it lights wet and burns a little hotter. I know they work well in damp weather because I have used them for decades. But homemade waterproof matches are not as wind resistant or as hot as commercial or military "storm matches". While a stick match flares 2-3 seconds, a storm match flares 10-15 seconds.

If you are in bad weather and really need a fire without screwing around, you want to have some military grade storm matches in your shirt pocket. If you can find them, try the NATO survival matches that come in a white can with 25 matches inside. The NSN is 9920-00-966-9432 and if your camping store does not sell them they are available online. If not, look for the kits made by UCO sold as survival matches or storm match kits; UCO has several good fire products.

Tinderbox

It is a very good idea to have a dry container for your tinder. Instead of wasting time looking for tinder before you need a fire, just collect it as you go and it will always be ready. If you plan to use flint & steel or fire pistons, the tinderbox is not really an option to decline.

It needs to be as water proof as it can be, small enough to carry easy in a pocket, large enough to hold tinder for several fires, and float if dropped in water. My answer is a $0.99 travel soap case. Other people often use old Skoal cans, snuff cans, large pill bottles, or very small cookie tins. You can even buy authentic brass tinderboxes for around $25. Either way whatever you use, a square one should be about 4"L x 2"W x 1"H and a round one about 3"W x 1.5"H.

Obviously you want to put tinder you come across throughout your day in your tinderbox for later. Starting off, things like steel wool, charcloth, cotton balls, and dryer lint should be in there. Other items may include some spare flint & steel or spare ferro rods. A tiny magnifying lens is smart. In my tinderboxes I keep a small pencil sharpener, like the ones kids use in school; any pencil sharpener is useful for turning twigs into tinder in a hurry.

I also tape a pair of P-38's or P-51's under the lid of my tinderboxes. These tiny can openers serve multiple uses. First, it ensures that within my pocket I always possess a way to open cans of food! It would be horrible to start a fire but not be able to open a can of chow. Second, sometimes you may want to cut an old coffee can or large soup can and modify it in to a disposable stove or suchlike.

Every bug-out bag or kit should include a tinderbox. I recommend every member of your group having one also.

18. Medical

This chapter is not meant to replace medical manuals. Always follow your doctor's advice. If you are injured or sick, get professional medical treatment if you can. I am not a doctor or civilian medical professional. I can only advise what I have learned in combat zones and disaster areas. My advice does not replace professional medical advice or care.

Training: If you are serious about survival, it makes sense to be as ready as you can be to treat a serious injury. A closet full of medical supplies is mostly useless without training.

Reading medical and first-aid books are alright. It is good to have that knowledge in your head or for reference. However! If you really think that you can learn enough to save your life (or anyone's life) just from reading a first aid book, you are a little unfamiliar with the real world.

Fixing a person with trauma is NOT the same as opening a maintenance manual and working on your truck. Medical and first-aid books (current books!) are good as references when caring for sick or recovering people, or for some refresher training, but that is the extent of their use.

Think about it: If you are on the ground going in shock from a gunshot wound, do you want the guys helping you that only know what they do from reading a manual or do you want guys helping you that have had hands-on training? You would at least hope they had taken an online class with video demonstrations and a test at the end!

Having said all that was not meant to insult anyone's intelligence. I mention it because so many survivalists I meet are woefully untrained or educated in extremely outdated first-aid techniques. But getting training is too easy to do. Nobody has to be outdated or untrained.

Classes- Organizations like the American Red Cross, National Safety Council (NSC), St. John's Ambulance, Boy Scouts, YMCA, and American Heart Association sponsor first-aid classes all over the US. Just about every modern country in the world has similar organizations. In fact, St. John's Ambulance and Red Cross are worldwide.

These classes, online, or classroom, are either free or low cost. Online classes that cost money average $20 to $110 (USD). Classroom classes that have fees are $60 to $150. Classroom time varies from 1 hour to 6 hours. That is not much time or money to get up to date first aid training. If online is not your style and you cannot attend classroom classes, you can order "training kits".

Do not overlook your community colleges. They offer first aid certification classes to meet employer or government (OSHA) safety requirements.

If you are not near a college, contact:

USA- American Safety and Health Institute (800.447.3177) Emergency Care and safety Institute (800-716-7264)

Australia- Australia Wide First Aid (1300 336 613)

Canada- Royal Life saving Society (416.490.8844) Canadian Ski Patrol (613.822.2245)

UK- Red Cross (0845 591 6192)

More extensive contacts for first aid training can be found by looking on your local/state Department of Human Services (DHS or DHHS) websites for their lists of acceptable training credentials for their providers.

Classes to consider:

- CPR
- AED (Often CPR &AED)
- Basic First Aid
- Infant/Child CPR (Pediatric)
- Infant/Child First Aid (Pediatric)
- Family First Aid
- Wilderness First Aid (Outdoor First Aid)
- Emergency Cardio
- Cardio Life Support
- Airborne & Bloodborne Pathogens
- Emergency Medical Response
- EpiPen & Anaphylaxes
- Sports First Aid
- Rescue First Aid

Prioritize which classes/training is most important to you when you are planning your overall disaster plan. Basic first aid will probably be the most useful to you in the beginning of a disaster. Knowing how to stop bleeding, open an airway, prevent/treat shock, treat fractures, treat burns, and CPR probably should get priority. A basic first aid class you took last weekend is better than the glamorous-sounding wilderness medical class you never take next summer.

Everyone needs basic first aid. Women may place more priority on pediatric first aid. Not every member in a group needs to know gunshot first aid or wilderness first aid right now if they do not know how to splint a broken bone or stabilize a spine injury yet. The point is, consider getting some basic schooling under your belt as soon as possible, and make it the right schooling.

Courses- Colleges, universities, institutes, and local companies offer courses. Whereas a class is just a few hours and is over in one or two days at most, courses can last several weeks. Distance learning is done online with proctored tests. Standard learning is done on campus. Most courses are made to fit around a workweek schedule, but some are full time.

Courses are made for people wanting or already have careers in emergency services or medicine. Nurses, assistants, caretakers, police/fire, paramedics, and first responders are among the professionals these classes are for. There are also schools for wilderness medicine that is meant for guides, trip leaders, professional hunters, explorers, instructors, and so forth.

Take a class or a real course? A few free classes are better than nothing and anybody can spare 10 hours a year for class. However, a few hours of training may not cover some topics long enough for you to retain the knowledge. Memory requires repetition. Also, if the student ratio is high in a class you are less likely to get hands-on practice in every topic. Courses take a lot more time and cost more money, but you will get more knowledge and remember it longer. Think of it this way: do you want your partner beside you in a fight to never have fired a weapon before? Would you hope he fired a gun for at least one weekend? You probably would prefer he trained with a gun for 14 weekend's right? Or maybe 100 weekends, right? It is the same concept with medical.

If you belong to a group or survival community, consider that you can pool money into a fund to send certain members of the group to medical/dental classes and courses over a prolonged period. With enough people and money, you may be able to cover dental, normal medical and wilderness medical simultaneously. Once proficient, those trained members can start acting both as the community medics and the trainers while they continue to move on to more advanced courses. Having people in your group currently trained in medicine vastly improves your odds in a long term catastrophe.

Also bear in mind you can recruit combat veteran medics or grow your own former military medics. By "grow your own", I mean have one or two members enlist for 3 years in the military as medics and afterwards bring that training home.

Manuals & Books- Books or manuals are great as a reference as long as you do not use them as a mental crutch to void real training. But they must be current!

Medical procedures at every level change every few years as new lessons are learned. It is a constantly evolving science.

For example: In OIF/OEF a lot of our guys bled to death because we did not know we were using tourniquet techniques that were obsolete. Up until as late as 2009 they were still training people to place tourniquets 2" below the nearest joint to save the joint. That sounds legit right? But below the elbow and knee it goes from one bone (Humerus or Femur) to two bones (Radius & Ulna or Tibia & Fibula). You can crank down a tourniquet until you strain yourself silly, but if it is around two bones, arterial blood will still keep flowing because those bones keep the compression of shutting severed arteries. Above the elbow or knee is one bone; thus a tourniquet can easily compress all the arteries closed. Obsolete first aid kills people.

All those Vietnam era military first aid manuals, still being sold, are trash. I say again, they are junk. Some of that stuff will get you or a family member killed. Those antique medical books, first aid books, and old Boy Scout first aid chapters that belonged to your parents when they were young should not be used.

When you buy first aid books or manuals, first verify the original publication date (not the release date) or the revision date. If it was published in 19xx, it is obsolete. From 2000-2006 is okay. Preferably purchase 2007 and up. As a general rule, I will not use a civilian manual more than 7 years old, or a military manual more than 15 years old.

Trauma: You probably have a few first aid kits. You may even have a stock of medical supplies, trauma kit, and a field surgery gear. I am not writing to explain how to remove an appendix or perform surgeries, but to briefly cover what is realistic in a real-world trauma kit intended for a disaster or post-apocalypse event.

First Aid Kit- These cost $10-$60 depending how much is in it. They are as small as a fiction novel or as large as a handbag. These are for **VERY MINOR** injuries. They are useful if you have a small cut or burn, a splinter, a headache, and other slight problems.

If you get shot, stabbed, fall, electrocuted, ran over, bludgeoned, flip a vehicle, caught on fire, hit by a brick, or anything along that level the regular first aid kit will not be much help.

So many times I have seen survivalists with those $10 kits in a camo pouch and think that is going to help. No way. What can you do for abdominal gunshot wounds or a severed limb with band-aids and a little roll of cotton tape? The answer is nothing.

The first aid kits have an important role but it is not for real trauma. Leave them around for things routine less significant injuries.

Improved First Aid Kit (IFAK) – This is a small pouch about the size of a thick novel that carries some individual trauma items. It is not meant to be a "do all" first aid kit. It contains just enough items to keep the victim alive until a medic arrives. When you come upon a casualty, you use his IFAK on him, not your own.

IFAK's contain a latex glove, one-way valve bandage, Israeli field dressing, a tourniquet (CAT), plastic airway (nasopharyngeal), medical tape roll, and combat gauze (blood clotting treated).

Notice there is no band-aids or little gauze packs in an IFAK.

The only thing I added to my IFAK was better tape and some meds. Medical tape is fine in a clean environment, but it is not good if blood, sweat, rain, dirt, or fluids are on the skin. You are better off with duct tape or electric tape. The meds I added was a baggy with a few doses of Tylenol, Motrin, caffeine, vitamin C, and vitamin B. The meds were in case I got separated and needed to stay alert for 24-48 hours until I found my way.

NOTE: Even though an IFAK has a tourniquet in it, our SOP was always 3 extra tourniquets per man. We attached the extras to our other gear. The reasoning was that it is not uncommon to require a tourniquet on 2 or 3, or even all 4 limbs. You can improvise a tourniquet most of the time, but it is a lot better to have a CAT, which is a very durable, simple, tourniquet with a plastic tightening bar (windless) built into it. We would race blindfolded in putting CATs on one-handed. Try that with conventional tourniquets! Also, over time the CAT has been improved; you can get it with a stronger metal bar and a better securing strap for the bar.

Combat Lifesaver Bag (CLS) - They are about the size of a hefty fanny pack/butt pack and cost from $100-$200 fully stocked. Older ones are OD Green and have a carrying strap. Newer ones are camo or tan and have both a strap and a MOLLE system. These bags are not used by medics. Every squad has one or two of these bags to care for wounded personnel until the actual medics can work to them.

CLS bags have a little bit of the routine items any first aid kit has. But it also has several IV bags, trauma needles, heavy shears, tourniquets, airways, moleskin, variety of large bandages, SAM splints, blood clot agent or combat gauze, possibly a blood expander agent, chest decompression needles, and etc.

Your CLS bag is where you begin to get into the life saving level of equipment. You have some of the tools you need to manipulate a victim's blood levels, respiration, and circulation.

Medic Aid Bag- This is the big bag you see medics humping everywhere they go. Fully stocked they will cost $200-$1,000. You can also get the EMT style bag or the mobile bins they use in ambulances and fire trucks.

The only level of care above these bags will have to come from an ambulance, aid station, and hospital. These bags typically have the tools to monitor vital signs. Rectal thermometer, oral thermometer, stethoscope, O2 sensor, and blood pressure at a minimum. There is enough supplies in a medic aid bag to prep casualties for transportation and evacuation to a place they can get better care.

Sustainment Care- Some supplies should be stored and cached for sustained care of injured members. It could take over a month for one person to recover. It would be wise to stock enough supplies to treat long-term injuries that occur in the onset of a disaster, and have enough supplies to treat more if anyone gets badly injured later.

Non-comprehensive list of useful clinic items:

- Large dressings (or diapers and maxi pads; cheaper and do same thing)
- Gauze rolls of assorted sizes (lots of gauze!)
- Gauze pads of assorted sizes
- Tampons
- Swabs
- Cotton rolls
- Medical tape (plastic, cloth, and porous)
- Duct Tape
- Soap, antibacterial
- Rags
- Hand sanitizer
- Sanitary wipes
- Latex gloves
- Disposable masks
- Blankets
- Razors (disposable shaving)
- Razor blades
- Iodine, Peroxide, and alcohol (lots and lots)

- Sodium chloride
- Butterfly dressings
- Pressure dressings
- Tefla bandages
- Antibiotic ointment
- Vaseline
- Burn ointments
- Medical glue
- Sutures
- Saline, bottled
- Chlorhexidine, bottled
- Saline IV, with lines and trauma needles
- Pediatric IV needles
- Chest decompression needles, 14GA
- One-way valve bandages
- Combat gauze
- Hextend
- Quick Clot
- Combat gauze
- Airways
- KY jelly
- Novocain, lidocaine
- Aspirin
- Ibuprofen
- Acetaminophen
- Antiseptic solution

- Pepto-Bismol
- Imodium
- EpiPen
- Benadryl
- Activated charcoal
- Hydration salts
- Caffeine citrate

There are a lot of drugs you need to decide whether to stock. Just remember that strong pain killer lower blood pressure, which can be fatal if there is blood loss. Seek proper training and education before handling or using prescription level drugs. Check the law to ensure what you plan to store is legal to have.

19. Trade goods

Nobody can make absolutely everything they need in the long-term. If money is useless, the currency will go back to precious metals, produce goods, textiles, and services. One way to get an edge up on this is to store extra of things you may want to use, but could easily trade as required. You want to store things that have a shelf life that is either indefinite or at least long enough to make a practical rotation schedule.

Apocalypse currency:

- <u>Salt</u>: It is worth more than gold.
- <u>Sugar</u>: White or brown. Highly trade-able item and stores indefinitely.
- <u>Honey</u>: Lots of nutrients and uses, and raw will last indefinitely.
- <u>Coffee</u>: Lasts 2 years.
- <u>Apple Cider Vinegar</u>: Lasts over a decade.
- <u>Black Pepper</u>: Lasts over a decade.

- <u>Tabasco & Worcestershire</u>: Lasts 5-10 years in cool storage.
- <u>Soap</u>: Most people cannot make it, thus it can become very valuable. Disease is the main killer in long term survival situations. Stock cases of bar soap.
- <u>Detergent powder</u>: Vacuum seal and store dry. Just think about the allure of clean clothes.
- <u>Liquors</u>: There will always be people willing to trade something for a drink. Spirits like brandy, whiskey, bourbon, vodka, gin, rum, and scotch will last over a century if unopened and kept in the dark.
- <u>Wine</u>: 3 years for grocery store wine. Indefinitely for the good stuff.
- <u>Tobacco</u>: More addictive than heroin and if vacuum sealed lasts a decade or more. Seeds are a good idea too. The seeds are cheap and easy to grow. Even if you do not smoke, you will be a wealthy individual from trading in even a small field of tobacco.

- <u>Razors and Toothbrushes</u>: Self explanatory. Buy a case of cheap ones.
- <u>Batteries</u>: Some alkaline have 10 years+ shelf lives. All lithium should last 10 years.
- <u>String</u>: Twine and thread are cheap but become a luxury once unavailable.
- <u>Toothpaste</u>: Self explanatory.
- <u>Scent</u>: Perfume, cologne, and aftershave.
- <u>Cloth</u>: Bundles of cheap cloth could eventually be pricey stuff.
- <u>Rope & Cord</u>: Most folks do not have any extra on hand.
- <u>Traps & Snares</u>: At some point furs and leather will be very valuable when no stores are selling new clothes. Furbearers and wild hogs are also a good meat source. Even if you do not want to do any trapping, the traps are a great trade item. Steel traps sell from $40-$200 a dozen based on size. Snares sell for around $15 a dozen. I by mine from Duke's or Oneida Victor; you can find them on EBay too.

- <u>Vitamins</u>: To supplement your diet if food is scarce.
- <u>Canned Food</u>: The canned food from the store can last a decade or more before the flavor is drastically changed. As long as the can holds up, the food is good. The Sell By Date on canned food is not dictated by safety or regulated by law (except baby formula). The manufacturers come up with those dates based on flavor change. They actually have experts who score the food based on flavor. After 1 year some vitamins start to diminish, but the nutrients stays the same. Century year old cans have been opened, tested, and found to be safe. Compare that to MREs, only 8 years max, or 5 years in unstable temperatures.
- <u>Seeds</u>: Keeping a variety of seeds is a great idea. Only save open-pollinated seeds. Hybrids will not correctly continue to come back. If dry stored, and kept refrigerated, you can keep seeds around 3-5 years

depending on species. And a jar full of seed packets can make a pretty big garden.

- <u>Nuts</u>: Plant some high yield nut trees like pecan, walnut, hickory, or whatever grows in your region. I prefer to put them on my property, but planting a few "secret groves" in other places can pay off. Every year you will get a crop of nuts to use or barter and with not much effort.
- <u>Fruit</u>: Plant some fruit tree orchards with a mix of apple, pear, plum, etc. Just like with nuts, every year you will have a crop of fruit to barter with, make wine, or whatever.
- <u>Mayonnaise</u>: Unopened stores indefinitely.

<u>Gold vs. Silver</u>- Having a little bit of gold stashed away is great. However, I caution against going overboard and buying too much of it. There are some problems with gold. First off, it is hard to know what gold is really worth because nobody has used it for currency in many years and our currencies are not even

backed by gold. An ounce of gold this year is about $1,350 USD average. A couple decades ago it was $2,400. In 1960, in today's dollars, it was about $200 an ounce.

So the question is, what will gold actually be worth after the economy collapses or civilization turns upside-down? Will an ounce of gold buy you ten horses or ten chickens? Will it buy a trailer full of wheat or a small basket of wheat? You can assume that after civilization picks itself back up a decade or a few decades after a catastrophe, gold will be worth a lot again. But nobody alive can really tell you an honest useable number. An ounce of gold may be a fortune or it may be worth a month's salary.

My concern is that you buy gold at over $1,000-$2,000 USD an ounce in today's dollar, but in a post-apocalypse economy it is worth about $40 an ounce. Look into what gold was worth in the 19th Century if you want to know what I mean. And $40 is a long way from $1,000.

The second issue with gold is difficulty in trading it for small purchases. Imagine if you get lucky and gold is worth a full $2,000 an ounce. Even if you break it into eighths, you have a $250 chunk to buy with. So, if you want to buy one thing for $20, you have to break that ounce down into hundredths. This type of thing could get insane if somehow gold became worth $20,000.

Silver is cheaper to buy. It currently sells at about $20 USD an ounce. Silver is great for making small purchases. Gold is great if you are buying a whole heard of cows, but silver is more practical if all you are buying is some chickens or a goat.

Another great thing about silver is it has antibacterial properties. You can put a silver dollar in a liquid like milk and it will stay fresh longer.